Bible Verses That Change Lives

Susie Johnson

TEACH Services, Inc.
P U B L I S H I N G
www.TEACHServices.com • (800) 367-1844

World rights reserved. This book or any portion thereof may not be copied or reproduced in any form or manner whatever, except as provided by law, without the written permission of the publisher, except by a reviewer who may quote brief passages in a review.

The author assumes full responsibility for the accuracy of all facts and quotations as cited in this book. The opinions expressed in this book are the author's personal views and interpretations, and do not necessarily reflect those of the publisher.

This book is provided with the understanding that the publisher is not engaged in giving spiritual, legal, medical, or other professional advice. If authoritative advice is needed, the reader should seek the counsel of a competent professional.

Copyright © 2019 Susie Johnson

Copyright © 2019 TEACH Services, Inc.

ISBN-13: 978-1-4796-1116-4 (Paperback)

ISBN-13: 978-1-4796-1117-1 (ePub)

Library of Congress Control Number: 2019907699

All Scripture references marked (KJV) are taken from the King James Version of the Bible. Public domain.

All Scripture references marked (NIV) are taken from the Holy Bible, New International Version®, NIV®, copyright © 1973, 1978, 1984, 2011 by Biblica, Inc.®. Used by permission. All rights reserved worldwide.

All Scripture references marked (NKJV) are taken from the New King James Version® of the Bible, copyright © 1982 by Thomas Nelson. Used by permission. All rights reserved.

All Scripture references marked (NRSV) are taken from the New Revised Standard Version Bible, copyright © 1989, the Division of Christian Education of the National Council of the Churches of Christ in the United States of America. Used by permission. All rights reserved.

All content is comprised of quotes from the Bible as indicated. The author has at times changed capitalization, and quotation marks have been omitted for readability.

Introduction

This book started as a topical list on anger, forgiveness, marriage, death, comfort, fear, baptism and many more subjects. What does the Bible say to those who are questioning their sexuality? Is hell real? I started by looking up Bible texts and putting them in my phone so I could look at them and share them with others. I spent three years collecting Bible verses. When at church, or during my personal worship time, whenever I read a text that had meaning to me, I added it to my growing list. I then decided I needed to organize it and print it. What you are now holding is the result of this effort.

    This book can be given to a sick friend or to someone who lost a loved one. It also can be used in a topical Bible study group, reading a chapter each week. What is the purpose of life? I believe that we are to devote our time to telling others the truths which are found in the Bible. When you see something amazing, don't you point and tell all around you? "Look at those dolphins at the bow of the boat!" Then you enjoy the experience together. It's the same thing when you give your heart to Jesus. You can't hold it in, and you want to tell friends, family, coworkers, and the person next to you on the plane! Put down your cellphone and talk to the people around you. Be loving and kind; give a friendly smile. Tell them Jesus loves them. Ask if you can pray for them or with them. Download the Bible on your phone, then when you look at your cellphone you will have something useful to read. Start reading a meaningful Bible verse out loud to the person next to you. The Bible is a timeless instruction book. It was relevant in Moses's time, and it is relevant today.

    Read with an open mind and a prayerful heart. Ask God for understanding and the Holy Spirit to work in your life and change you from the inside. Those around you will see the change and will realize that you have come to know Jesus as your personal Savior. When you are done with this little book, don't stop there. Read your Bible. Start in Matthew and read through to Revelation, then start in Genesis and read to the end of Revelation again. If you get bogged down in any chapter, then go back to Matthew. Study your Bible, if you think of a subject you want to know more about—then look up every verse that has anything to do with that subject. Don't just read that verse; read the verses around it, even the whole chapter for more clarification. Let the Bible be its own interpreter.

If you feel lacking in your life and you are bored, volunteer somewhere and get involved in a church. Join a Bible study group or a prayer group or start a Bible study group of your own. Live your life like Jesus is coming today. Plus, keep working like it's going to be a hundred years. We need to live like Jesus is coming tomorrow because it might be tomorrow for us. We are not guaranteed to live until old age. Every day is a gift from God. Live your life as a witness to those around you. We are living in the last days of this earth's history. You can see it in the earthquakes, not only increasing in frequency but also in strength, tornados, and other natural disasters, and turmoil in the country and our government. We need to be ready to meet our Savior. We need to wake up every day with a prayer to Jesus for strength to make it through another day. When life gets tough, stop and say a quick prayer. God is always listening. He's waiting for you to ask Him for help. Won't you give your life to Him?

I ask God to give you understanding of the passages you read and a thirst to get to know Him better. I want every one of my family and friends in heaven with me. If I don't know you, then I want to meet you in heaven where we can be friends throughout eternity! He loves you and so do I, even if I have not met you yet!

Dear Jesus, please send Your Holy Spirit to work on the hearts of each person who reads this book or any portion of it. Give to all an open mind and a prayerful heart. Forgive us our sins. We love You, Jesus. Amen.

Praying that I will meet YOU in heaven,
Susie Johnson

Table of Contents

Chapter 1: Your Word is Truth 7
Chapter 2: War Broke out in Heaven 10
Chapter 3: Have Faith in God 13
Chapter 4: Do Not Fret—It Only Causes Harm 16
Chapter 5: May the Lord Give You Increase 19
Chapter 6: Two are Better than One 24
Chapter 7: Train up a Child 28
Chapter 8: Do Not Enter the Path of the Wicked 32
Chapter 9: Baptized into Christ 40
Chapter 10: You Are My Witnesses 42
Chapter 11: Remember the Sabbath Day 48
Chapter 12: Flee Sexual Immorality 51
Chapter 13: Forgive, and You Will Be Forgiven 57
Chapter 14: Is Anyone Among You Sick? 61
Chapter 15: The Dead Know Nothing 64
Chapter 16: You Will Have Tribulation 67
Chapter 17: Fear Not for I Am with You 72
Chapter 18: The Day Which is Coming Shall Burn Them Up 76
Chapter 19: Therefore Pray 79
Chapter 20: He is Coming with Clouds 82

Chapter 1: Your Word is Truth

The entirety of Your word is truth, And every one of Your righteous judgments endures forever. Psalms 119:160, NKJV.

In the beginning was the Word, and the Word was with God, and the Word was God. John 1:1, NKJV.

By the word of the Lord were the heavens made; and all the host of them by the breath of His mouth. For He spake, and it was done; He commanded, and it stood fast. Psalms 33:6, 9, KJV.

All things were made by Him; and without Him was not any thing made that was made. John 1:3, KJV.

Know ye that the Lord He is God: it is He that hath made us, and not we ourselves; we are His people, and the sheep of His pasture. Psalms 100:3, KJV.

In whose hand is the soul of every living thing, and the breath of all mankind. Job 12:10, KJV.

You are worthy, our Lord and God, to receive glory and honor and power, for You created all things, and by Your will they were created and have their being. Revelation 4:11, NIV.

Search the scriptures; for in them ye think ye have eternal life: and they are they which testify of Me. John 5:39, KJV.

And the Word became flesh and dwelt among us, and we beheld His glory, the glory as of the only begotten of the Father, full of grace and truth. John 1:14, NKJV.

Nor is there salvation in any other, for there is no other name under heaven given among men by which we must be saved. Acts 4:12, NKJV.

In hope of eternal life, which God, that cannot lie, promised before the world began. Titus 1:2, KJV.

Jesus answered them, and said, My doctrine is not Mine, but His that sent Me. If any man will do His will, he shall know of the doctrine, whether it be of God, or whether I speak of Myself. John 7:16, 17, KJV.

Father, I desire that they also whom You gave Me may be with Me where I am, that they may behold My glory which You have given Me; for You loved Me before the foundation of the world. John 17:24, NKJV.

All Scripture is given by inspiration of God, and is profitable for doctrine, for reproof, for correction, for instruction in righteousness, that the man of God may be complete, thoroughly equipped for every good work. 2 Timothy 3:16, 17, NKJV.

Every word of God is pure: He is a shield unto them that put their trust in Him. Proverbs 30:5, KJV.

My son, if you accept my words and store up my commands within you, turning your ear to wisdom and applying your heart to understanding — indeed, if you call out for insight and cry aloud for understanding, and if you look for it as for silver and search for it as for hidden treasure, then you will understand the fear of the Lord, and find the knowledge of God. For the Lord gives wisdom; from His mouth come knowledge and understanding. He holds success in store for the upright, He is a shield to those whose walk is blameless, for He guards the course of the just and protects the way of His faithful ones. Then you will understand what is right and just and fair—every good path. For wisdom will enter your heart, and knowledge will be pleasant to your soul. Discretion will protect you, and understanding will guard you. Wisdom will save you from the ways of wicked men, from men whose words are perverse. Proverbs 2:1–12, NIV.

Thy word is a lamp unto my feet, and a light unto my path. Psalms 119:105, KJV.

These were more fair-minded ... in that they received the word with all readiness, and searched the Scriptures daily to find out whether these things were so. Acts 17:11, NKJV.

Therefore, get rid of all moral filth and the evil that is so prevalent and humbly accept the word planted in you, which can save you. James 1:21, NIV.

For whatsoever things were written aforetime were written for our learning, that we through patience and comfort of the Scriptures might have hope. Romans 15:4, KJV.

We also have the prophetic message as something completely reliable, and you will do well to pay attention to it, as to a light shining in a dark place, until the day dawns and the morning star rises in your hearts. Above all, you must understand that no prophecy of Scripture came about by the prophet's own interpretation of things. For prophecy never had its origin in the human will, but prophets, though human, spoke from God as they were carried along by the Holy Spirit. 2 Peter 1:19–21, NIV.

For this cause also thank we God without ceasing, because, when ye received the word of God which ye heard of us, ye received it not as the word of men, but as it is in truth, the word of God, which effectually worketh also in you that believe. 1 Thessalonians 2:13, KJV.

The words of the Lord are pure words: as silver tried in a furnace of earth, purified seven times. Thou shalt keep them, O Lord, thou shalt preserve them from this generation for ever. Psalms 12:6, 7, KJV.

Think not that I am come to send peace on earth: I came not to send peace, but a sword. Matthew 10:34, KJV.

For the word of God is alive and active. Sharper than any double-edged sword, it penetrates even to dividing soul and spirit, joints and marrow; it judges the thoughts and attitudes of the heart. Nothing in all creation is hidden from God's sight. Everything is uncovered and laid bare before the eyes of Him to whom we must give account. Hebrews 4:12, 13, NIV.

Heaven and earth shall pass away, but My words shall not pass away. Matthew 24:35, KJV.

Sanctify them through Thy truth: Thy word is truth. John 17:17, KJV.

Chapter 2: War Broke out in Heaven

And war broke out in heaven: Michael and his angels fought with the dragon; and the dragon and his angels fought, but they did not prevail, nor was a place found for them in heaven any longer. So the great dragon was cast out, that serpent of old, called the Devil and Satan, who deceives the whole world; he was cast to the earth, and his angels were cast out with him. Revelation 12:7–9, NKJV.

How art thou fallen from heaven, O Lucifer, son of the morning! how art thou cut down to the ground, which didst weaken the nations! For thou hast said in thine heart, I will ascend into heaven, I will exalt my throne above the stars of God: I will sit also upon the mount of the congregation, in the sides of the north: I will ascend above the heights of the clouds; I will be like the Most High. Isaiah 14:12–14, KJV.

Now the serpent was more cunning than any beast of the field which the Lord God had made. And he said to the woman, "Has God indeed said, 'You shall not eat of every tree of the garden'?" And the woman said to the serpent, "We may eat the fruit of the trees of the garden; but of the fruit of the tree which is in the midst of the garden, God has said, 'You shall not eat it, nor shall you touch it, lest you die.' " Then the serpent said to the woman, "You will not surely die. For God knows that in the day you eat of it your eyes will be opened, and you will be like God, knowing good and evil." So when the woman saw that the tree was good for food, that it was pleasant to the eyes, and a tree desirable to make one wise, she took of its fruit and ate. She also gave to her husband with her, and he ate. Genesis 3:1–6, NKJV.

Be sober, be vigilant; because your adversary the devil, as a roaring lion, walketh about, seeking whom he may devour. 1 Peter 5:8, KJV.

Jesus said to him, "Away from me, Satan! For it is written: 'Worship the Lord your God, and serve Him only.' " Matthew 4:10, NIV.

Therefore submit to God. Resist the devil and he will flee from you. Draw near to God and He will draw near to you. Cleanse your hands, you sinners; and purify your hearts, you double-minded. Humble yourselves in the sight of the Lord, and He will lift you up. James 4:7, 8, 10, NKJV.

Love must be sincere. Hate what is evil; cling to what is good. Be devoted to one another in love. Honor one another above yourselves. Never be lacking in zeal, but keep your spiritual fervor, serving the Lord. Be joyful in hope, patient in affliction, faithful in prayer. Share with the Lord's people who are in need. Practice hospitality. Romans 12:9–13, NIV.

For there is one God, and one Mediator between God and men, the Man Christ Jesus; Who gave Himself a ransom for all, to be testified in due time. 1 Timothy 2:5, 6, KJV.

Therefore, just as through one man sin entered the world, and death through sin, and thus death spread to all men, because all sinned— But the free gift is not like the offense. For if by the one man's offense many died, much more the grace of God and the gift by the grace of the one Man, Jesus Christ, abounded to many. For if by the one man's offense death reigned through the one, much more those who receive abundance of grace and of the gift of righteousness will reign in life through the One, Jesus Christ. Therefore, as through one man's offense judgment came to all men, resulting in condemnation, even so through one Man's righteous act the free gift came to all men, resulting in justification of life. For as by one man's disobedience many were made sinners, so also by one Man's obedience many will be made righteous. Romans 5:12, 15, 17–19, NKJV.

But now Christ is risen from the dead, and has become the firstfruits of those who have fallen asleep. For since by man came death, by Man also came the resurrection of the dead. For as in Adam all die, even so in Christ all shall be made alive. 1 Corinthians 15:20–22, NKJV.

Finally, my brethren, be strong in the Lord, and in the power of His might. Put on the whole armour of God, that ye may be able to stand against the wiles of the devil. For we wrestle not against flesh and blood, but against principalities, against powers, against the rulers of the darkness of this world, against spiritual wickedness in the high places. Wherefore take unto you the whole armour of God, that ye may be able to withstand in the evil day, and having done all, to stand. Stand therefore, having your loins girt about with truth, and having on the breastplate of righteousness; And your feet shod with the preparation of the gospel of peace; Above all, taking the shield of faith, wherewith ye shall be able to quench all the fiery darts of the wicked. And take the helmet of salvation, and the sword of the Spirit, which is the word of God: Praying always with all prayer and supplication in the Spirit, and watching thereunto with all perseverance and supplication for all saints; And for me, that utterance may be given unto me, that I may open my mouth boldly, to make known the mystery of the gospel, For which I am an ambassador in bonds: that therein I may speak boldly, as I ought to speak. Ephesians 6:10–20, KJV.

For the Son of Man is come to seek and to save that which was lost. Luke 19:10, KJV.

Chapter 3: Have Faith in God

So Jesus answered and said to them, "Have faith in God. For assuredly, I say to you, whoever says to this mountain, 'Be removed and be cast into the sea,' and does not doubt in his heart, but believes that those things he says will be done, he will have whatever he says. Therefore I say to you, whatever things you ask when you pray, believe that you receive them, and you will have them." Mark 11:22–24, NKJV.

Now faith is the substance of things hoped for, the evidence of things not seen. Hebrews 11:1, KJV.

For we were saved in this hope, but hope that is seen is not hope; for why does one still hope for what he sees? But if we hope for what we do not see, we eagerly wait for it with perseverance. Romans 8:24, 25, NKJV.

For by grace are ye saved through faith; and that not of yourselves: it is the gift of God: Not of works, lest any man should boast. Ephesians 2:8, 9, KJV.

But when the kindness and the love of God our Savior toward man appeared, not by works of righteousness which we have done, but according to His mercy He saved us, through the washing of regeneration and renewing of the Holy Spirit, whom He poured out on us abundantly through Jesus Christ our Savior, that having been justified by His grace we should become heirs according to the hope of eternal life. Titus 3:4–7, NKJV.

Whosoever shall confess that Jesus is the Son of God, God dwelleth in him, and he in God. 1 John 4:15, KJV.

Then Jesus said to her, "Woman, you have great faith! Your request is granted." And her daughter was healed at that moment. Matthew 15:28, NIV.

Very truly I tell you, whoever believes in Me will do the works I have been doing, and they will do even greater things than these, because I am going to the Father. John 14:12, NIV.

For therein is the righteousness of God revealed from faith to faith: as it is written, The just shall live by faith. Romans 1:17, KJV.

But let all those rejoice who put their trust in You; Let them ever shout for joy, because You defend them; Let those also who love Your name Be joyful in You. For you, O Lord, will bless the righteous; With favor You will surround him as with a shield. Psalms 5:11, 12, NKJV.

… "With men it is impossible, but not with God; for with God all things are possible." Mark 10:27, NKJV.

Let us hold fast to the confession of our hope without wavering, for he who has promised is faithful. Hebrews 10:23, NRSV.

Because if you confess with your lips that Jesus is Lord and believe in your heart that God raised Him from the dead, you will be saved. For one believes with the heart and so is justified, and one confesses with the mouth and so is saved. The scripture says, "No one who believes in Him will be put to shame." For there is no distinction between Jew and Greek; the same Lord is Lord of all and is generous to all who call on Him. For, "Everyone who calls on the name of the Lord shall be saved." Romans 10:9–13, NRSV.

But someone will say, "You have faith, and I have works." Show me your faith without your works, and I will show you my faith by my works. You believe that there is one God. You do well. Even the demons believe—and tremble! But do you want to know, O foolish man, that faith without works is dead? For as the body without the spirit is dead, so faith without works is dead also. James 2:18–20, 26, NKJV.

Therefore being justified by faith, we have peace with God through our Lord Jesus Christ: By whom also we have access by faith into this grace wherein we stand, and rejoice in hope of the glory of God. Romans 5:1, 2, KJV.

Though He slay me, yet will I trust Him. Even so, I will defend my own ways before Him. Job 13:15, NKJV.

For we live by faith, not by sight. 2 Corinthians 5:7, NIV.

Trust in the Lord with all your heart, And lean not on your own understanding; In all your ways acknowledge Him, And He shall direct your paths. Proverbs 3:5, 6, NKJV.

And my speech and my preaching was not with enticing words of man's wisdom, but in demonstration of the Spirit and of power: That your faith should not stand in the wisdom of men, but in the power of God. 1 Corinthians 2:4, 5, KJV.

I am crucified with Christ: nevertheless I live; yet not I, but Christ liveth in me: and the life which I now live in the flesh I live by the faith of the Son of God, who loved me, and gave Himself for me. Galatians 2:20, KJV.

I tell you this so that no one may deceive you by fine-sounding arguments. For though I am absent from you in body, I am present with you in spirit and delight to see how disciplined you are and how firm your faith in Christ is. Colossians 2:4, 5, NIV.

And Moses said to the people, "Do not be afraid. Stand still, and see the salvation of the Lord, which He will accomplish for you today. For the Egyptians whom you see today, you shall see again no more forever. The Lord will fight for you, and you shall hold your peace." Exodus 14:13, 14, NKJV.

As for God, His way is perfect; The word of the Lord is proven; He is a shield to all who trust in Him. Psalms 18:30, NKJV.

So then faith cometh by hearing, and hearing by the word of God. Romans 10:17, KJV.

Jesus said to him, "If you can believe, all things are possible to him who believes." Immediately the father of the child cried out and said with tears, "Lord, I believe; help my unbelief!" Mark 9:23, 24, NKJV.

Chapter 4: Do Not Fret—It Only Causes Harm

Rest in the Lord, and wait patiently for Him; Do not fret because of him who prospers in his way, Because of the man who brings wicked schemes to pass. Cease from anger, and forsake wrath; Do not fret—it only causes harm. For evildoers shall be cut off; But those who wait on the Lord, They shall inherit the earth. For yet a little while and the wicked shall be no more; Indeed, you will look carefully for his place, But it shall be no more. But the meek shall inherit the earth, And shall delight themselves in the abundance of peace. Psalms 37:7–11, NKJV.

By contrast, the fruit of the Spirit is love, joy, peace, patience, kindness, generosity, faithfulness, gentleness, and self-control. There is no law against such things. Galatians 5:22, 23, NRSV.

He that is slow to wrath is of great understanding: but he that is hasty of spirit exalteth folly. Proverbs 14:29, KJV.

Be angry, and do not sin. Meditate within your heart on your bed, and be still. Psalms 4:4, NKJV.

A soft answer turns away wrath, But a harsh word stirs up anger. The tongue of the wise uses knowledge rightly, But the mouth of fools pours forth foolishness. Proverbs 15:1, 2, NKJV.

Bless those who persecute you; bless and do not curse them. Rejoice with those who rejoice, weep with those who weep. Live in harmony with one another; do not be haughty, but associate with the lowly; do not claim to be wiser than you are. Do not repay anyone evil for evil, but take thought for what is noble in the sight of all. If it is possible, so far as it depends on you, live peaceably with all. Beloved, never avenge yourselves, but leave room for the wrath of God; for it is written, "Vengeance is Mine, I will repay, says the Lord." No, "if your enemies are hungry, feed them; if they are thirsty, give them something to drink; for by doing this you will heap burning coals on their heads." Do not be overcome by evil, but overcome evil with good. Romans 12:14–21, NRSV.

For the mountains shall depart, and the hills be removed; but My kindness shall not depart from thee, neither shall the covenant of My peace be removed, saith the Lord that hath mercy on thee. Isaiah 54:10, KJV.

The wise are cautious and turn away from evil, but the fool throws off restraint and is careless. One who is quick-tempered acts foolishly, and the schemer is hated. Proverbs 14:16, 17, NRSV.

For his anger is but for a moment; his favor is for a lifetime. Weeping may linger for the night, but joy comes with the morning. Psalms 30:5, NRSV.

Better a small serving of vegetables with love than a fattened calf with hatred. A hot-tempered person stirs up conflict, but the one who is patient calms a quarrel. Proverbs 15:17, 18, NIV.

It is better to dwell in the wilderness, than with a contentious and an angry woman. Proverbs 21:19, KJV.

A cheerful heart is a good medicine, but a downcast spirit dries up the bones. Proverbs 17:22, NRSV.

Pursue peace with all people, and holiness, without which no one will see the Lord: looking carefully lest anyone fall short of the grace of God; lest any root of bitterness springing up cause trouble, and by this many become defiled. Hebrews 12:14, 15, NKJV.

Be not hasty in thy spirit to be angry: for anger resteth in the bosom of fools. Ecclesiastes 7:9, KJV.

Be ye angry, and sin not: let not the sun go down upon your wrath: Neither give place to the devil. Let all bitterness, and wrath, and anger, and clamor, and evil speaking, be put away from you, with all malice: And be ye kind one to another, tenderhearted, forgiving one another, even as God for Christ's sake hath forgiven you. Ephesians 4:26, 27, 31, 32, KJV.

Every wise woman buildeth her house: but the foolish plucketh it down with her hands. Proverbs 14:1, KJV.

Wherefore, my beloved brethren, let every man be swift to hear, slow to speak, slow to wrath: For the wrath of man worketh not the righteousness of God. James 1:19, 20, KJV.

Beloved, let us love one another: for love is of God; and every one that loveth is born of God, and knoweth God. He that loveth not knoweth not God; for God is love. 1 John 4:7, 8, KJV.

He that hath knowledge spareth his words: and a man of understanding is of an excellent spirit. Even a fool, when he holdeth his peace, is counted wise: and he that shutteth his lips is esteemed a man of understanding. Proverbs 17:27, 28, KJV.

But now ye also put off all these; anger, wrath, malice, blasphemy, filthy communication out of your mouth. Colossians 3:8, KJV.

Chapter 5: May the Lord Give You Increase

May the Lord give you increase more and more, You and your children. May you be blessed by the Lord, Who made heaven and earth. Psalms 115:14, 15, NKJV.

But thou shalt remember the Lord thy God: for it is He that giveth thee power to get wealth, that He may establish His covenant which He sware unto thy fathers, as it is this day. Deuteronomy 8:18, KJV.

The earth is the Lord's, and the fulness thereof; the world, and they that dwell therein. Psalms 24:1, KJV.

The silver is Mine, and the gold is Mine, saith the Lord of hosts. Haggai 2:8, KJV.

Command those who are rich in this present age not to be haughty, nor to trust in uncertain riches but in the living God, who gives us richly all things to enjoy. Let them do good, that they be rich in good works, ready to give, willing to share, storing up for themselves a good foundation for the time to come, that they may lay hold on eternal life. 1 Timothy 6:17–19, NKJV.

Let your conversation be without covetousness; and be content with such things as ye have: for He hath said, I will never leave thee, nor forsake thee. So that we may boldly say, The Lord is my helper, and I will not fear what man shall do unto me. Hebrews 13:5, 6, KJV.

... "Render therefore to Caesar the things that are Caesar's, and to God the things that are God's." Matthew 22:21, NKJV.

Pay to all what is due them—taxes to whom taxes are due, revenue to whom revenue is due, respect to whom respect is due, honor to whom honor is due. Owe no one anything, except to love one another; for the one who loves another has fulfilled the law. Romans 13:7, 8, NRSV.

But godliness with contentment is great gain. 1 Timothy 6:6, KJV.

And if thou draw out thy soul to the hungry, and satisfy the afflicted soul; then shall thy light rise in obscurity, and thy darkness be as the noonday: And the Lord shall guide thee continually, and satisfy thy soul in drought, and make fat thy bones: and thou shalt be like a watered garden, and like a spring of water, whose waters fail not. Isaiah 58:10, 11, KJV.

For every beast of the forest is Mine, and the cattle upon a thousand hills. Psalms 50:10, KJV.

O fear the Lord, ye His saints: for there is no want to them that fear Him. The young lions do lack, and suffer hunger: but they that seek the Lord shall not want any good thing. Psalms 34:9, 10, KJV.

Therefore do not be like them. For your Father knows the things you have need of before you ask Him. Matthew 6:8, NKJV.

And my God shall supply all your need according to His riches in glory by Christ Jesus. Philippians 4:19, NKJV.

Better is little with the fear of the Lord than great treasure and trouble therewith. Proverbs 15:16, KJV.

Anyone who tills the land will have plenty of bread, but one who follows worthless pursuits will have plenty of poverty. The faithful will abound with blessings, but one who is in a hurry to be rich will not go unpunished. To show partiality is not good—yet for a piece of bread a person may do wrong. The miser is in a hurry to get rich and does not know that loss is sure to come. Proverbs 28:19–22, NRSV.

For even when we were with you, this we commanded you, that if any would not work, neither should he eat. For we hear that there are some which walk among you disorderly, working not at all, but are busybodies. 2 Thessalonians 3:10, 11, KJV.

Go to the ant, you sluggard! Consider her ways and be wise, Which, having no captain, Overseer or ruler, Provides her supplies in the summer, And gathers her food in the harvest. How long will you slumber, O sluggard? When will you rise from your sleep? A little sleep, a little slumber, A little folding of the hands to sleep—So shall your poverty come on you like a prowler, And your need like an armed man. Proverbs 6:6–11, NKJV.

Let him that stole steal no more: but rather let him labour, working with his hands the thing which is good, that he may have to give to him that needeth. Ephesians 4:28, KJV.

Neither is worshiped with men's hands, as though He needed any thing, seeing He giveth to all life, and breath, and all things. Acts 17:25, KJV.

And He said unto them, Take heed, and beware of covetousness: for man's life consisteth not in the abundance of the things which he possesseth. Luke 12:15, KJV.

There is one who scatters, yet increases more; And there is one who withholds more than is right, But it leads to poverty. Proverbs 11:24, NKJV.

My son, if you become surety for your friend, If you have shaken hands in pledge for a stranger, You are snared by the words of your mouth; You are taken by the words of your mouth. So do this, my son, and deliver yourself; For you have come into the hand of your friend: Go and humble yourself; Plead with your friend. Give no sleep to your eyes, Nor slumber to your eyelids. Deliver yourself like a gazelle from the hand of the hunter, And like a bird from the hand of the fowler. Proverbs 6:1-5, NKJV.

Do not be one of those who shakes hands in a pledge, One of those who is surety for debts; If you have nothing with which to pay, Why should he take away your bed from under you? Proverbs 22:26, 27, NKJV.

The rich rules over the poor, And the borrower is servant to the lender. Proverbs 22:7, NKJV.

He who is surety for a stranger will suffer, But one who hates being surety is secure. Proverbs 11:15, NKJV.

Jesus looked at him and said, "How hard it is for the rich to enter the kingdom of God! Indeed, it is easier for a camel to go through the eye of a needle than for someone who is rich to enter the kingdom of God." Those who heard this asked, "Who then can be saved?" Jesus replied, "What is impossible with man is possible with God." Luke 18:24–27, NIV.

Ye have sown much, and bring in little; ye eat, but ye not have enough; ye drink, but ye are not filled with drink; ye clothe you, but there is none warm; and he that earneth wages earneth wages to put it into a bag with holes. Ye looked for much, and, lo, it came to little; and when ye brought it home, I did blow upon it. Why? saith the Lord of hosts. Because of Mine house that is waste, and ye run every man unto his own house. Therefore the heaven over you is stayed from dew, and the earth is stayed from her fruit. And I called for a drought upon the land, and upon the mountains, and upon the corn, and upon the new wine, and upon the oil, and upon that which the ground bringeth forth, and upon men, and upon cattle, and upon all the labour of the hands. Haggai 1:6, 9–11, KJV.

Will a man rob God? Yet ye have robbed Me. But ye say, Wherein have we robbed Thee? In tithes and offerings. Ye are cursed with a curse: for ye have robbed Me, even this whole nation. Bring ye all the tithes into the storehouse, that there may be meat in Mine house, and prove Me now herewith, saith the Lord of hosts, if I will not open you the windows of heaven, and pour you out a blessing, that there shall not be room enough to receive it. And I will rebuke the devourer for your sakes, and he shall not destroy the fruits of your ground; neither shall your vine cast her fruit before the time in the field, saith the Lord of hosts. And all nations shall call you blessed: for ye shall be a delightsome land, saith the Lord of hosts. Malachi 3:8–12, KJV.

Honor the Lord with your possessions, And with the firstfruits of all your increase; So your barns will be filled with plenty, And your vats will overflow with new wine. Proverbs 3:9, 10, NKJV.

Every man shall give as he is able, according to the blessing of the Lord thy God which He hath given thee. Deuteronomy 16:17, KJV.

So now I bring the first of the fruit of the ground that you, O Lord, have given me. You shall set it down before the Lord your God and bow down before the Lord your God. Deuteronomy 26:10, NRSV.

Then all Judah brought the tithe of the grain, wine, and oil into the storehouses. Nehemiah 13:12, NRSV.

Give unto the Lord the glory due unto His name: bring an offering, and come into His courts. Psalms 96:8, KJV.

Trust not in oppression, and become not vain in robbery: if riches increase, set not your heart upon them. Psalms 62:10, KJV.

Cast but a glance at riches, and they are gone, for they will surely sprout wings and fly off to the sky like an eagle. Proverbs 23:5, NIV.

They that trust in their wealth, and boast themselves in the multitude of their riches; None of them can by any means redeem his brother, nor give to God a ransom for him. Psalms 49:6, 7, KJV.

But this I say, He which soweth sparingly shall reap also sparingly; and he which soweth bountifully shall reap also bountifully. Every man according as he purposeth in his heart, so let him give; not grudgingly, or of necessity: for God loveth a cheerful giver. 2 Corinthians 9:6, 7, KJV.

Give, and it will be given to you: good measure, pressed down, shaken together, and running over will be put into your bosom. For with the same measure that you use, it will be measured back to you. Luke 6:38, NKJV.

Do not lay up for yourselves treasures on earth, where moth and rust destroy and where thieves break in and steal; but lay up for yourselves treasures in heaven, where neither moth nor rust destroys and where thieves do not break in and steal. For where your treasure is, there your heart will be also. Matthew 6:19–21, NKJV.

For we brought nothing into this world, and it is certain we can carry nothing out. And having food and clothing, with these we shall be content. But those who desire to be rich fall into temptation and a snare, and into many foolish and harmful lusts which drown men in destruction and perdition. For the love of money is a root of all kinds of evil, for which some have strayed from the faith in their greediness, and pierced themselves through with many sorrows. 1 Timothy 6:7–10, NKJV.

Chapter 6: Two are Better than One

Two are better than one, Because they have a good reward for their labor. For if they fall, one will lift up his companion. But woe to him who is alone when he falls, For he has no one to help him up. Again, if two lie down together, they will keep warm; But how can one be warm alone? Though one may be overpowered by another, two can withstand him. And a threefold cord is not quickly broken. Ecclesiastes 4:9–12, NKJV.

And the Lord God said, "It is not good that man should be alone; I will make him a helper comparable to him." Genesis 2:18, NKJV.

And the rib, which the Lord God had taken from man, made He a woman, and brought her unto the man. And Adam said, This is now bone of my bones, and flesh of my flesh: she shall be called Woman, because she was taken out of Man. Therefore shall a man leave his father and his mother, and shall cleave unto his wife: and they shall be one flesh. Genesis 2:22–24, KJV.

So God created man in His own image, in the image of God created He him; male and female created He them. And God blessed them, and God said unto them, Be fruitful, and multiply, and replenish the earth, and subdue it: and have dominion over the fish of the sea, and over the fowl of the air, and over every living thing that moveth upon the earth. Genesis 1:27, 28, KJV.

Now to the married I command, yet not I but the Lord: A wife is not to depart from her husband. But even if she does depart, let her remain unmarried or be reconciled to her husband. And a husband is not to divorce his wife. But to the rest I, not the Lord, say: If any brother has a wife who does not believe, and she is willing to live with him, let him not divorce her. And a woman who has a husband who does not believe, if he is willing to live with her, let her not divorce him. For the unbelieving husband is sanctified by the wife, and the unbelieving wife is sanctified by the husband; otherwise your children would be unclean, but now they are holy. But if the unbeliever departs, let him depart; a brother or a sister is not under bondage in such cases. But God has called us to peace. For how do you know, O wife, whether you will save your husband? Or how do you know, O husband, whether you will save your wife? 1 Corinthians 7:10–16, NKJV.

Wives, submit yourselves unto your own husbands, as unto the Lord. For the husband is the head of the wife, even as Christ is the head of the church: and He is the Savior of the body. Therefore as the church is subject unto Christ, so let the wives be to their own husbands in every thing. Husbands, love your wives, even as Christ also loved the church, and gave Himself for it. So ought men to love their wives as their own bodies. He that loveth his wife loveth himself. For this cause shall a man leave his father and mother, and shall be joined unto his wife, and they two shall be one flesh. Nevertheless let every one of you in particular so love his wife even as himself; and the wife see that she reverence her husband. Ephesians 5:22–25, 28, 31, 33, KJV.

Husbands, in the same way, show consideration for your wives in your life together, paying honor to the woman as the weaker sex, since they too are also heirs of the gracious gift of life—so that nothing may hinder your prayers. Finally, all of you, have unity of spirit, sympathy, love for one another, a tender heart, and a humble mind. Do not repay evil for evil or abuse for abuse; but, on the contrary, repay with a blessing. It is for this that you were called—that you might inherit a blessing. 1 Peter 3:7-9, NRSV.

A wife of noble character who can find? She is worth far more than rubies. Her husband has full confidence in her and lacks nothing of value. She brings him good, not harm, all the days of her life. She is clothed with strength and dignity; she can laugh at the days to come. She speaks with wisdom, and faithful instruction is on her tongue. She watches over the affairs of her household and does not eat the bread of idleness. Her children arise and call her blessed; her husband also, and he praises her: "Many women do noble things, but you surpass them all." Charm is deceptive, and beauty is fleeting; but a woman who fears the Lord is to be praised. Honor her for all that her hands have done, and let her works bring her praise at the city gate. Proverbs 31:10–12, 25–31, NIV.

"They say, 'If a man divorces his wife, And she goes from him And becomes another man's, May he return to her again?' Would not that land be greatly polluted? But you have played the harlot with many lovers; Yet return to Me," says the Lord. Jeremiah 3:1, NKJV.

When a man takes a wife and marries her, and it happens that she finds no favor in his eyes because he has found some uncleanness in her, and he writes her a certificate of divorce, puts it in her hand, and sends her out of his house, when she has departed from his house, and goes and becomes another man's wife, if the latter husband detests her and writes her a certificate of divorce, puts it in her hand, and sends her out of his house, or if the latter husband dies who took her as his wife, then her former husband who divorced her must not take her back to be his wife after she has been defiled; for that is an abomination before the Lord, and you shall not bring sin on the land which the Lord your God is giving you as an inheritance. Deuteronomy 24:1–4, NKJV.

Yet you say, "For what reason?" Because the Lord has been witness Between you and the wife of your youth, With whom you have dealt treacherously; Yet she is your companion And your wife by covenant. But did He not make them one, Having a remnant of the Spirit? And why one? He seeks godly offspring. Therefore take heed to your spirit, And let none deal treacherously with the wife of his youth. "For the Lord God of Israel says That He hates divorce, For it covers one's garment with violence," Says the Lord of hosts. "Therefore take heed to your spirit, That you do not deal treacherously." Malachi 2:14–16, NKJV.

Do not cast me away when I am old; do not forsake me when my strength is gone. Psalms 71:9, NIV.

For the woman which hath an husband is bound by the law to her husband so long as he liveth; but if the husband be dead, she is loosed from the law of her husband. So then if, while her husband liveth, she be married to another man, she shall be called an adulteress: but if her husband be dead, she is free from that law; so that she is no adulteress, though she be married to another man. Romans 7:2, 3, KJV.

Let nothing be done through selfish ambition or conceit, but in lowliness of mind let each esteem others better than himself. Let each of you look out not only for his own interests, but also for the interests of others. Philippians 2:3, 4, NKJV.

Your wife shall be like a fruitful vine In the very heart of your house, Your children like olive plants All around your table. Behold, thus shall the man be blessed Who fears the Lord. Psalms 128:3, 4, NKJV.

Let the husband render to his wife the affection due her, and likewise also the wife to her husband. The wife does not have authority over her own body, but the husband does. And likewise the husband does not have authority over his own body, but the wife does. Do not deprive one another except with consent for a time, that you may give yourselves to fasting and prayer; and come together again so that Satan does not tempt you because of your lack of self-control. 1 Corinthians 7:3–5, NKJV.

Anyone who divorces his wife and marries another woman commits adultery, and the man who marries a divorced woman commits adultery. Luke 16:18, NIV.

"And I say to you, whoever divorces his wife, except for sexual immorality, and marries another, commits adultery; and whoever marries her who is divorced commits adultery." His disciples said to Him, "If such is the case of the man with his wife, it is better not to marry." But He said to them, "All cannot accept this saying, but only those to whom it has been given: For there are eunuchs who were born thus from their mother's womb, and there are eunuchs who were made eunuchs by men, and there are eunuchs who have made themselves eunuchs for the kingdom of heaven's sake. He who is able to accept it, let him accept it." Matthew 19:9–12, NKJV.

Do not be yoked together with unbelievers. For what do righteousness and wickedness have in common? Or what fellowship can light have with darkness? What harmony is there between Christ and Belial? Or what does a believer have in common with an unbeliever? What agreement is there between the temple of God and idols? For we are the temple of the living God. As God has said: "I will live with them and walk among them, and I will be their God, and they will be My people." 2 Corinthians 6:14–16, NIV.

Though I speak with the tongues of men and of angels, but have not love, I have become sounding brass or a clanging cymbal. And though I have the gift of prophecy, and understand all mysteries and all knowledge, and though I have all faith, so that I could remove mountains, but have not love, I am nothing. And though I bestow all my goods to feed the poor, and though I give my body to be burned, but have not love, it profits me nothing. Love suffers long and is kind; love does not envy; love does not parade itself, is not puffed up; does not behave rudely, does not seek its own, is not provoked, thinks no evil; does not rejoice in iniquity, but rejoices in the truth; bears all things, believes all things, hopes all things, endures all things. But when that which is perfect has come, then that which is in part will be done away. When I was a child, I spoke as a child, I understood as a child, I thought as a child; but when I became a man, I put away childish things. For now we see in a mirror, dimly, but then face to face. Now I know in part, but then I shall know just as I also am known. And now abide faith, hope, love, these three; but the greatest of these is love.
1 Corinthians 13:1-7, 10-13, NKJV.

Chapter 7: Train up a Child

Train up a child in the way he should go, And when he is old he will not depart from it. Proverbs 22:6, NKJV.

For You created my inmost being; You knit me together in my mother's womb. I praise You because I am fearfully and wonderfully made; Your works are wonderful, I know that full well. My frame was not hidden from you when I was made in the secret place, when I was woven together in the depths of the earth. Your eyes saw my unformed body; all the days ordained for me were written in your book before one of them came to be. Psalms 139:13–16, NIV.

Behold, children are a heritage from the Lord, The fruit of the womb is a reward. Like arrows in the hand of a warrior, So are the children of one's youth. Happy is the man who has his quiver full of them; They shall not be ashamed, But shall speak with their enemies in the gate. Psalms 127:3–5, NKJV.

Father of orphans and protector of widows is God in His holy habitation. Psalms 68:5, NRSV.

Can a woman forget her sucking child, that she should not have compassion on the son of her womb? yea, they may forget, yet will I not forget thee. Behold, I have graven thee upon the palms of My hands; thy walls are continually before Me. Isaiah 49:15, 16, KJV.

He that loveth father or mother more than Me is not worthy of Me: and he that loveth son or daughter more than Me is not worthy of Me. Matthew 10:37, KJV.

Whoever spares the rod hates their children, but the one who loves their children is careful to discipline them. Proverbs 13:24, NIV.

Foolishness is bound up in the heart of a child; The rod of correction will drive it far from him. Proverbs 22:15, NKJV.

Endure hardship as discipline; God is treating you as His children. For what children are not disciplined by their father? If you are not disciplined—and everyone undergoes discipline—then you are not legitimate, not true sons and daughters at all. Moreover, we have all had human fathers who disciplined us and we respected them for it. How much more should we submit to the Father of spirits and live! They disciplined us for a little while as they thought best; but God disciplines us for our good, in order that we may share in His holiness. No discipline seems pleasant at the time, but painful. Later on, however, it produces a harvest of righteousness and peace for those who have been trained by it. Hebrews 12:7–11, NIV.

Children, obey your parents in the Lord, for this is right. "Honor your father and mother"—this is the first commandment with a promise: "so that it may be well with you and you may live long on the earth." And, fathers, do not provoke your children to anger, but bring them up in the discipline and instruction of the Lord. Ephesians 6:1–4, NRSV.

Flee the evil desires of youth and pursue righteousness, faith, love and peace, along with those who call on the Lord out of a pure heart. 2 Timothy 2:22, NIV.

Even children make themselves known by their acts, by whether what they do is pure and right. Proverbs 20:11, NRSV.

… Serve the Lord! And if it seems evil to you to serve the Lord, choose for yourselves this day whom you will serve … But as for me and my house, we will serve the Lord. Joshua 24:14, 15, NKJV.

And all thy children shall be taught of the Lord; and great shall be the peace of thy children. Isaiah 54:13, KJV.

And if anyone gives even a cup of cold water to one of these little ones who is my disciple, truly I tell you, that person will certainly not lose their reward. Matthew 10:42, NIV.

Children, obey your parents in all things: for this is well pleasing unto the Lord. Fathers, provoke not your children to anger, lest they be discouraged. Colossians 3:20, 21, KJV.

My son, do not despise the chastening of the Lord, Nor detest His correction; For whom the Lord loves He corrects, Just as a father the son in whom he delights. Happy is the man who finds wisdom, And the man who gains understanding. Do not withhold good from those to whom it is due, When it is in the power of your hand to do so. Proverbs 3:11–13, 27, NKJV.

Do all things without murmurings and disputings: That ye may be blameless and harmless, the sons of God, without rebuke, in the midst of a crooked and perverse nation, among whom ye shine as lights in the world; Holding forth the word of life; that I may rejoice in the day of Christ, that I have not run in vain, neither laboured in vain. Philippians 2:14–16, KJV.

Fix these words of mine in your hearts and minds; tie them as symbols on your hands and bind them on your foreheads. Teach them to your children, talking about them when you sit at home and when you walk along the road, when you lie down and when you get up. Write them on the doorframes of your houses and on your gates, so that your days and the days of your children may be many in the land the Lord swore to give your ancestors, as many as the days that the heavens are above the earth. Deuteronomy 11:18–21, NIV.

But thus says the Lord: "Even the captives of the mighty shall be taken away, And the prey of the terrible be delivered; For I will contend with him who contends with you, And I will save your children." Isaiah 49:25, NKJV.

Children's children are the crown of old men; and the glory of children are their fathers. Proverbs 17:6, KJV.

For I will pour water upon him that is thirsty, and floods upon the dry ground: I will pour My Spirit upon thy seed, and My blessing upon thine offspring. Isaiah 44:3, KJV.

People were bringing little children to Jesus for Him to place His hands on them, but the disciples rebuked them. When Jesus saw this, He was indignant. He said to them, "Let the little children come to Me, and do not hinder them, for the kingdom of God belongs to such as these. Truly I tell you, anyone who will not receive the kingdom of God like a little child will never enter it." And He took the children in His arms, placed His hands on them and blessed them. Mark 10:13–16, NIV.

They replied, "Believe in the Lord Jesus, and you will be saved—you and your household." Acts 16:31, NIV.

This is what the Lord says: "Restrain your voice from weeping and your eyes from tears, for your work will be rewarded," declares the Lord. "They will return from the land of the enemy. So there is hope for your descendants," declares the Lord. "Your children will return to their own land." Jeremiah 31:16, 17, NIV.

Then Jesus called a little child to Him, set him in the midst of them, and said, "Assuredly, I say to you, unless you are converted and become as little children, you will by no means enter the kingdom of heaven. Therefore whoever humbles himself as this little child is the greatest in the kingdom of heaven. Whoever receives one little child like this in My name receives Me." Matthew 18:2–5, NKJV.

Chapter 8: Do Not Enter the Path of the Wicked

Do not enter the path of the wicked, And do not walk in the way of evil. Avoid it, do not travel on it; Turn away from it and pass on. For they do not sleep unless they have done evil; And their sleep is taken away unless they make someone fall. For they eat the bread of wickedness, And drink the wine of violence. But the path of the just is like the shining sun, That shines ever brighter unto the perfect day. The way of the wicked is like darkness; They do not know what makes them stumble. My son, give attention to my words; Incline your ear to my sayings. Do not let them depart from your eyes; Keep them in the midst of your heart; For they are life to those who find them, And health to all their flesh. Keep your heart with all diligence, For out of it spring the issues of life. Put away from you a deceitful mouth, And put perverse lips far from you. Let your eyes look straight ahead, And your eyelids look right before you. Ponder the path of your feet, And let all your ways be established. Do not turn to the right or the left; Remove your foot from evil. Proverbs 4:14–27, NKJV.

See that no one renders evil for evil to anyone, but always pursue what is good both for yourselves and for all. 1 Thessalonians 5:15, NKJV.

Above all, my beloved, do not swear, either by heaven or by earth or by any other oath, but let your "Yes" be yes and your "No" be no, so that you may not fall under condemnation. James 5:12, NRSV.

Watch and pray, lest you enter into temptation. The spirit indeed is willing, but the flesh is weak. Matthew 26:41, NKJV.

He who covers his sins will not prosper, But whoever confesses and forsakes them will have mercy. Proverbs 28:13, NKJV.

Oh Lord, correct me, but with justice; Not in Your anger, lest You bring me to nothing. Jeremiah 10:24, NKJV.

Who desires everyone to be saved and to come to the knowledge of the truth. 1 Timothy 2:4, NRSV.

Wine is a mocker, strong drink is raging: and whoever is deceived thereby is not wise. Proverbs 20:1, KJV.

But Daniel purposed in his heart that he would not defile himself with the portion of the king's meat, nor with the wine which he drank: therefore he requested of the prince of the eunuchs that he might not defile himself. Daniel 1:8, KJV.

Be not among winebibbers; among riotous eaters of flesh: For the drunkard and the glutton shall come to poverty: and drowsiness shall clothe a man with rags. Proverbs 23:20, 21, KJV.

Brethren, if anyone among you wanders from the truth, and someone turns him back, let him know that he who turns a sinner from the error of his way will save a soul from death and cover a multitude of sins. James 5:19, 20, NKJV.

Do not be misled: "Bad company corrupts good character." Come back to your senses as you ought, and stop sinning; for there are some who are ignorant of God—I say this to your shame. 1 Corinthians 15:33, 34, NIV.

Make no friendship with an angry man, And with a furious man do not go, Lest you learn his ways And set a snare for your soul. Proverbs 22:24, 25, NKJV.

Lie not one to another, seeing that ye have put off the old man with his deeds. Colossians 3:9, KJV.

Do not desire her beauty in your heart, and do not let her capture you with her eyelashes; for a prostitute's fee is only a loaf of bread, but the wife of another stalks a man's very life. Can fire be carried in the bosom without burning one's clothes? Or can one walk on hot coals without scorching the feet? So is he who sleeps with his neighbor's wife; no one who touches her will go unpunished. Proverbs 6:25-29, NRSV.

For I know the thoughts that I think toward you, says the Lord, thoughts of peace and not of evil, to give you a future and a hope. Then you will call upon Me and go and pray to Me, and I will listen to you. And you will seek Me and find Me, when you search for Me with all your heart. Jeremiah 29:11-13, NKJV.

But fornication and all uncleanness or covetousness, let it not even be named among you, as is fitting for saints; neither filthiness, nor foolish talking, nor course jesting, which are not fitting, but rather giving of thanks. For this you know, that no fornicator, unclean person, nor covetous man, who is an idolater, has any inheritance in the kingdom of Christ and God. Let no one deceive you with empty words, for because of these things the wrath of God comes upon the sons of disobedience. Therefore do not be partakers with them. Ephesians 5:3–7, NKJV.

Repent ye therefore, and be converted, that your sins may be blotted out, when the times of refreshing shall come from the presence of the Lord. Acts 3:19, KJV.

By this we know that we love the children of God, when we love God and keep His commandments. For this is the love of God, that we keep His commandments. And His commandments are not burdensome. 1 John 5:2, 3, NKJV.

I, even I, am He that blotteth out thy transgressions for Mine own sake, and will not remember thy sins. Isaiah 43:25, KJV.

In like manner also, that the women adorn themselves in modest apparel, with propriety and moderation, not with braided hair or gold or pearls or costly clothing, but, which is proper for women professing godliness, with good works. 1 Timothy 2:9, 10, NKJV.

Ye shall not make any cuttings in your flesh for the dead, nor tattoo any marks on you: I am the Lord. Leviticus 19:28, NKJV.

Therefore submit to God. Resist the devil and he will flee from you. Draw near to God and He will draw near to you. Cleanse your hands, you sinners; and purify your hearts, you double-minded. James 4:7, 8, NKJV.

Enter through the narrow gate; for the gate is wide and the road is easy that leads to destruction, and there are many who take it. For the gate is narrow and the road is hard that leads to life, and there are few who find it. Matthew 7:13, 14, NRSV.

Seek the Lord while He may be found, Call upon Him while He is near. Let the wicked forsake his way, And the unrighteous man his thoughts; Let him return to the Lord, And He will have mercy on him; And to our God, for He will abundantly pardon. Isaiah 55:6, 7, NKJV.

Jesus answered, "Those who are well have no need of a physician, but those who are sick; I have come to call not the righteous but sinners to repentance." Luke 5:31, 32, NRSV.

My son, forget not my law; but let thine heart keep my commandments: For length of days, and long life, and peace, shall they add to thee. Proverbs 3:1, 2, KJV.

Therefore let him who thinks he stands take heed lest he fall. No temptation has overtaken you except such as is common to man; but God is faithful, who will not allow you to be tempted beyond what you are able, but with the temptation will also make the way of escape, that you may be able to bear it. 1 Corinthians 10:12, 13, NKJV.

Pride goes before destruction, and a haughty spirit before a fall. Proverbs 16:18, NRSV.

… With men it is impossible, but not with God; for with God all things are possible. Mark 10:27, NKJV.

We do not dare to classify or compare ourselves with some who commend themselves. When they measure themselves by themselves and compare themselves with themselves, they are not wise. 2 Corinthians 10:12, NIV.

But the wisdom from above is first pure, then peaceable, gentle, willing to yield, full of mercy and good fruits, without a trace of partiality or hypocrisy. James 3:17, NRSV.

But avoid foolish controversies and genealogies and arguments and quarrels about the law, because these are unprofitable and useless. Warn a divisive person once, and then warn them a second time. After that, have nothing to do with them. You may be sure that such people are warped and sinful; they are self-condemned. Titus 3:9-11, NIV.

Wait on the Lord; Be of good courage, And He shall strengthen your heart; Wait, I say, on the Lord! Psalms 27:14, NKJV.

I will instruct you and teach you in the way you should go; I will guide you with My eye. Psalms 32:8, NKJV.

I said, "I will guard my ways, Lest I sin with my tongue; I will restrain my mouth with a muzzle, While the wicked are before me." Psalms 39:1, NKJV.

... Truly, the fear of the Lord, that is wisdom; and to depart from evil is understanding. Job 28:28, NRSV.

These six things the Lord hates, Yes, seven are an abomination to Him: A proud look, A lying tongue, Hands that shed innocent blood, A heart that devises wicked plans, Feet that are swift in running to evil, A false witness who speaks lies, And one who sows discord among brethren. Proverbs 6:16-19, NKJV.

Blessed is the man that endureth temptation: for when he is tried, he shall receive the crown of life, which the Lord hath promised to them that love Him. Let no man say when he is tempted, I am tempted of God: for God cannot be tempted with evil, neither tempteth He any man: But every man is tempted, when he is drawn away of his own lust, and enticed. Then when lust hath conceived, it bringeth forth sin: and sin, when it is finished, bringeth forth death. James 1:12–15, KJV.

You shall love the Lord your God with all your heart, with all your soul, and with all your strength. And these words which I command you today shall be in your heart. You shall teach them diligently to your children, and shall talk of them when you sit in your house, when you walk by the way, when you lie down, and when you rise up. You shall bind them as a sign on your hand, and they shall be as frontlets between your eyes. You shall write them on the doorposts of your house and on your gates. Deuteronomy 6:5–9, NKJV.

What then? Shall we sin because we are not under law but under grace? Certainly not! Romans 6:15, NKJV.

Have mercy upon me, O God, according to thy lovingkindness: according unto the multitude of thy tender mercies blot out my transgressions. Wash me thoroughly from mine iniquity, and cleanse me from my sin. For I acknowledge my transgressions: and my sin is ever before me. Psalms 51:1–3, KJV.

Everyone who commits sin is guilty of lawlessness; sin is lawlessness. 1 John 3:4, NRSV.

Blessed is he whose transgression is forgiven, Whose sin is covered. Blessed is the man to whom the Lord does not impute iniquity, And in whose spirit there is no deceit. Psalms 32:1, 2, NKJV.

The Lord is slow to anger, and great in power, and will not at all acquit the wicked: the Lord hath His way in the whirlwind and in the storm, and the clouds are the dust of His feet. Nahum 1:3, KJV.

"Wash yourselves, make yourselves clean; Put away the evil of your doings from before My eyes. Cease to do evil, Learn to do good; Seek justice, Rebuke the oppressor; Defend the fatherless, Plead for the widow. Come now, and let us reason together," Says the Lord, "Though your sins are like scarlet, They shall be as white as snow; Though they are red like crimson, They shall be as wool. If you are willing and obedient, You shall eat the good of the land; But if you refuse and rebel, You shall be devoured by the sword"; For the mouth of the Lord has spoken. Isaiah 1:16–20, NKJV.

If we say that we have no sin, we deceive ourselves, and the truth is not in us. If we confess our sins, He is faithful and just to forgive us our sins and to cleanse us from all unrighteousness. 1 John 1:8, 9, NKJV.

And whatsoever we ask, we receive of Him, because we keep His commandments, and do those things that are pleasing in His sight. 1 John 3:22, KJV.

Behold, the Lord's hand is not shortened, that it cannot save; neither His ear heavy, that it cannot hear: But your iniquities have separated between you and your God, and your sins have hid His face from you, that He will not hear. Isaiah 59:1, 2, KJV.

If any of you lacks wisdom, let him ask of God, who gives to all liberally and without reproach, and it will be given to him. James 1:5, NKJV.

Jesus answered them, "Most assuredly, I say to you, whoever commits sin is a slave of sin. And a slave does not abide in the house forever, but a son abides forever. Therefore if the Son makes you free, you shall be free indeed." John 8:34–36, NKJV.

Here is a trustworthy saying that deserves full acceptance: Christ Jesus came into the world to save sinners—of whom I am the worst. 1 Timothy 1:15, NIV.

You will say, "Branches were broken off so that I might be grafted in." That is true. They were broken off because of their unbelief, but you stand only through faith. So do not become proud, but stand in awe. For if God did not spare the natural branches, perhaps He will not spare you. Note then the kindness and severity of God: severity toward those who have fallen, but God's kindness toward you, provided you continue in his kindness; otherwise you also will be cut off. And even those of Israel, if they do not persist in unbelief, will be grafted in, for God has the power to graft them in again. For if you have been cut from what is by nature a wild olive tree and grafted, contrary to nature, into a cultivated olive tree, how much more will these natural branches be grafted back into their own olive tree. Romans 11:19–24, NRSV.

Seeing then that we have a great High Priest, that is passed into the heavens, Jesus the Son of God, let us hold fast our profession. For we have not an High Priest which cannot be touched with the feeling of our infirmities; but was in all points tempted like as we are, yet without sin. Let us therefore come boldly unto the throne of grace, that we may obtain mercy, and find grace to help in time of need. Hebrews 4:14–16, KJV.

Let every soul be subject to the governing authorities. For there is no authority except from God, and the authorities that exist are appointed by God. Romans 13:1, NKJV.

You shall have no other gods before Me. You shall not make for yourself a carved image, or any likeness of anything that is in heaven above, or that is in the earth beneath, or that is in the water under the earth; you shall not bow down to them nor serve them. For I, the Lord your God, am a jealous God, visiting the iniquity of the fathers on the children to the third and fourth generations of those who hate Me, but showing mercy to thousands, to those who love Me and keep My commandments. You shall not take the name of the Lord your God in vain, for the Lord will not hold him guiltless who takes His name in vain. Remember the Sabbath day, to keep it holy. Six days you shall labor and do all your work, but the seventh day is the Sabbath of the Lord your God. In it you shall do no work: you, nor your son, nor your daughter, nor your male servant, nor your female servant, nor your cattle, nor your stranger who is within your gates. For in six days the Lord made the heavens and the earth, the sea, and all that is in them, and rested the seventh day. Therefore the Lord blessed the Sabbath day and hallowed it. Honor your father and your mother, that your days may be long upon the land which the Lord your God is giving you. You shall not murder. You shall not commit adultery. You shall not steal. You shall not bear false witness against your neighbor. You shall not covet your neighbor's house; you shall not covet your neighbor's wife, nor his male servant, nor his female servant, nor his ox, nor his donkey, nor anything that is your neighbor's. Exodus 20:3–17, NKJV.

And I will cleanse them from all their iniquity, whereby they have sinned against Me; and I will pardon all their iniquities, whereby they have sinned, and whereby they have transgressed against Me. Jeremiah 33:8, KJV.

For all have sinned, and come short of the glory of God; Being justified freely by His grace through the redemption that is in Christ Jesus. Romans 3:23, 24, KJV.

As long as my breath is in me, And the breath of God in my nostrils, My lips will not speak wickedness, Nor my tongue utter deceit. Job 27:3, 4, NKJV.

Yet in all these things we are more than conquerors through Him who loved us. For I am persuaded that neither death nor life, nor angels nor principalities nor powers, nor things present nor things to come, nor height nor depth, nor any other created thing, shall be able to separate us from the love of God which is in Christ Jesus our Lord. Romans 8:37–39, NKJV.

Because you have kept My command to persevere, I also will keep you from the hour of trial which shall come upon the whole world, to test those who dwell on the earth. Behold, I am coming quickly! Hold fast what you have, that no one may take your crown. Revelation 3:10, 11, NKJV.

Chapter 9: Baptized into Christ

Or do you not know that as many of us as were baptized into Christ Jesus were baptized into His death? Therefore we were buried with Him through baptism into death, that just as Christ was raised from the dead by the glory of the Father, even so we also should walk in newness of life. For if we have been united together in the likeness of His death, certainly we also shall be in the likeness of His resurrection, knowing this, that our old man was crucified with Him, that the body of sin might be done away with, that we should no longer be slaves of sin. Romans 6:3–6, NKJV.

Then Jesus came from Galilee to John at the Jordan, to be baptized by him. John would have prevented Him, saying, "I need to be baptized by You, and do You come to me?" But Jesus answered him, "Let it be so now; for it is proper for us in this way to fulfill all righteousness." Then he consented. Matthew 3:13–15, NRSV.

It came to pass in those days that Jesus came from Nazareth of Galilee, and was baptized by John in the Jordan. And immediately, coming up from the water, He saw the heavens parting and the Spirit descending upon Him like a dove. Then a voice came from heaven, "You are My beloved Son, in whom I am well pleased." Mark 1:9–11, NKJV.

Jesus answered, "Very truly I tell you, no one can enter the kingdom of God unless they are born of water and the Spirit." John 3:5, NIV.

The one who believes and is baptized will be saved; but the one who does not believe will be condemned. Mark 16:16, NRSV.

But as many as received Him, to them gave He power to become the sons of God, even to them that believe on His name. John 1:12, KJV.

Then Peter said unto them, Repent, and be baptized every one of you in the name of Jesus Christ for the remission of sins, and ye shall receive the gift of the Holy Ghost. For the promise is unto you, and to your children, and to all that are afar off, even as many as the Lord our God shall call. Acts 2:38, 39, KJV.

And he commanded the chariot to stand still: and they went down both into the water, both Philip and the eunuch; and he baptized him. Acts 8:38, KJV.

Having been buried with Him in baptism, in which you were also raised with Him through your faith in the working of God, who raised Him from the dead. Colossians 2:12, NIV.

One Lord, one faith, one baptism. Ephesians 4:5, KJV.

And now why are you waiting? Arise and be baptized, and wash away your sins, calling on the name of the Lord. Acts 22:16, NKJV.

Listen! I am standing at the door, knocking; if you hear My voice and open the door, I will come in to you and eat with you, and you with Me. Revelation 3:20, NRSV.

Jesus said to him, "I am the way, and the truth, and the life. No one comes to the Father except through Me." John 14:6, NRSV.

For as many of you as have been baptized into Christ have put on Christ. Galatians 3:27, KJV.

Go ye therefore, and teach all nations, baptizing them in the name of the Father, and of the Son, and of the Holy Ghost: Teaching them to observe all things whatsoever I have commanded you: and, lo, I am with you alway, even unto the end of the world. Amen. Matthew 28:19, 20, KJV.

Chapter 10: You Are My Witnesses

"You are My witnesses," says the Lord, "and My servant whom I have chosen, that you may know and believe Me, And understand that I am He. Before Me there was no God formed, Nor shall there be after Me. I, even I, am the Lord, And besides Me there is no savior. I have declared and saved, I have proclaimed, And there was no foreign god among you; Therefore you are My witnesses," Says the Lord, "that I am God. This people I have formed for Myself; They shall declare My praise." Isaiah 43:10–12, 21, NKJV.

Preach the word! Be ready in season and out of season. Convince, rebuke, exhort, with all longsuffering and teaching. For the time will come when they will not endure sound doctrine, but according to their own desires, because they have itching ears, they will heap up for themselves teachers; and they will turn their ears away from the truth, and be turned aside to fables. But you be watchful in all things, endure afflictions, do the work of an evangelist, fulfill your ministry. 2 Timothy 4:2–5, NKJV.

Also I heard the voice of the Lord, saying, Whom shall I send, and who will go for us? Then said I, Here am I; send me. Isaiah 6:8, KJV.

How then shall they call on Him in whom they have not believed? And how shall they believe in Him of whom they have not heard? And how shall they hear without a preacher? And how shall they preach unless they are sent? As it is written: "How beautiful are the feet of those who preach the gospel of peace, Who bring glad tidings of good things!" Romans 10:14, 15, NKJV.

Brethren, if a man be overtaken in a fault, ye which are spiritual, restore such an one in the spirit of meekness; considering thyself, lest thou also be tempted. Bear ye one another's burdens, and so fulfil the law of Christ. Galatians 6:1, 2, KJV.

Even so the Lord has commanded that those who preach the gospel should live from the gospel. 1 Corinthians 9:14, NKJV.

And whatever you do, do it heartily, as to the Lord and not to men, knowing that from the Lord you will receive the reward of the inheritance, for you serve the Lord Christ. Colossians 3:23, 24, NKJV.

A new commandment I give unto you, That ye love one another; as I have loved you, that ye also love one another. By this shall all men know that ye are My disciples, if ye have love one to another. John 13:34, 35, KJV.

He gives power to the weak, And to those who have no might He increases strength. Even the youths shall faint and be weary, And the young men shall utterly fall, But those who wait on the Lord shall renew their strength; They shall mount up with wings like eagles, They shall run and not be weary, They shall walk and not faint. Isaiah 40:29–31, NKJV.

If you abide in Me, and My words abide in you, you will ask what you desire, and it shall be done for you. By this My Father is glorified, that you bear much fruit; so you will be My disciples. John 15:7, 8, NKJV.

And He said unto me, My grace is sufficient for thee: for My strength is made perfect in weakness. Most gladly therefore will I rather glory in my infirmities, that the power of Christ may rest upon me. Therefore I take pleasure in infirmities, in reproaches, in necessities, in persecutions, in distresses for Christ's sake: for when I am weak, then I am strong. 2 Corinthians 12:9, 10, KJV.

For the body is not one member, but many. 1 Corinthians 12:14, KJV.

And the Lord make you to increase and abound in love one toward another, and toward all men, even as we do toward you. 1 Thessalonians 3:12, KJV.

Brethren, if anyone among you wanders from the truth, and someone turns him back, let him know that he who turns a sinner from the error of his way will save a soul from death and cover a multitude of sins. James 5:19, 20, NKJV.

Now John answered and said, "Master, we saw someone casting out demons in Your name, and we forbade him because he does not follow with us." But Jesus said to him, "Do not forbid him, for he who is not against us is on our side." Now it came to pass, when the time had come for Him to be received up, that He steadfastly set His face to go to Jerusalem, and sent messengers before His face. And as they went, they entered a village of the Samaritans, to prepare for Him. But they did not receive Him, because His face was set for the journey to Jerusalem. And when His disciples James and John saw this, they said, "Lord, do You want us to command fire to come down from heaven and consume them, just as Elijah did?" But He turned and rebuked them, and said, "You do not know what manner of spirit you are of. For the Son of Man did not come to destroy men's lives but to save them." And they went to another village. Luke 9:49–56, NKJV.

Give no regard to mediums and familiar spirits; do not seek after them, to be defiled by them: I am the Lord your God. Leviticus 19:31, NKJV.

There shall not be found among you anyone who makes his son or his daughter pass through the fire, or one who practices witchcraft, or a soothsayer, or one who interprets omens, or a sorcerer, or one who conjures spells, or a medium, or a spiritist, or one who calls up the dead. For all who do these things are an abomination to the Lord, and because of these abominations the Lord your God drives them out from before you. Deuteronomy 18:10-12, NKJV.

Rather, that the things which the Gentiles sacrifice they sacrifice to demons and not to God, and I do not want you to have fellowship with demons. 1 Corinthians 10:20, NKJV.

To the law and to the testimony: if they speak not according to this word, it is because there is no light in them. Isaiah 8:20, KJV.

Whom will he teach knowledge? And whom will he make to understand the message? Those just weaned from milk? Those just drawn from the breasts? For precept must be upon precept, precept upon precept, Line upon line, line upon line, Here a little, there a little. Isaiah 28:9, 10, NKJV.

Do not despise the words of prophets, but test everything; hold fast to what is good; abstain from every form of evil. 1 Thessalonians 5:20–22, NRSV.

Surely the Lord God does nothing, without revealing His secret to His servants the prophets. Amos 3:7, NRSV.

Beloved, do not believe every spirit, but test the spirits, whether they are of God; because many false prophets have gone out into the world. By this you know the Spirit of God: Every spirit that confesses that Jesus Christ has come in the flesh is of God, and every spirit that does not confess that Jesus Christ has come in the flesh is not of God. And this is the spirit of the Antichrist, which you have heard was coming, and is now already in the world. 1 John 4:1–3, NKJV.

The prophet which prophesieth of peace, when the word of the prophet shall come to pass, then shall the prophet be known, that the Lord hath truly sent him. Jeremiah 28:9, KJV.

Then said Jesus to those Jews which believed on Him, If ye continue in My word, then are ye My disciples indeed; And ye shall know the truth, and the truth shall make you free. John 8:31, 32, KJV.

Beware of false prophets, which come to you in sheep's clothing, but inwardly they are ravening wolves. Ye shall know them by their fruits. Do men gather grapes of thorns, or figs of thistles? Even so every good tree bringeth forth good fruit; but a corrupt tree bringeth forth evil fruit. A good tree cannot bring forth evil fruit, neither can a corrupt tree bring forth good fruit. Every tree that bringeth not forth good fruit is hewn down, and cast into the fire. Wherefore by their fruits ye shall know them. Matthew 7:15–20, KJV.

Then I saw another angel flying in the midst of heaven, having the everlasting gospel to preach to those who dwell on the earth—to every nation, tribe, tongue, and people—saying with a loud voice, "Fear God and give glory to Him, for the hour of His judgment has come; and worship Him who made heaven and earth, the sea and springs of water." Revelation 14:6, 7, NKJV.

And another angel followed, saying, "Babylon is fallen, is fallen, that great city, because she has made all nations drink of the wine of the wrath of her fornication." Then a third angel followed them, saying with a loud voice, "If anyone worships the beast and his image, and receives his mark on his forehead or on his hand, he himself shall also drink of the wine of the wrath of God, which is poured out full strength into the cup of His indignation. He shall be tormented with fire and brimstone in the presence of the holy angels and in the presence of the Lamb. And the smoke of their torment ascends forever and ever; and they have no rest day or night, who worship the beast and his image, and whoever receives the mark of his name." Revelation 14:8–11, NKJV.

For this reason I also suffer these things; nevertheless I am not ashamed, for I know whom I have believed and am persuaded that He is able to keep what I have committed to Him until that Day. 2 Timothy 1:12, NKJV.

And ye shall be hated of all men for My name's sake: but he that shall endure unto the end, the same shall be saved. Mark 13:13, KJV.

Call upon Me in the day of trouble; I will deliver you, and you shall glorify Me. Psalms 50:15, NKJV.

And I fell at his feet to worship him. And he said unto me, See thou do it not: I am thy fellowservant, and of thy brethren that have the testimony of Jesus: worship God: for the testimony of Jesus is the spirit of prophecy. Revelation 19:10, KJV.

I can do all things through Christ which strengtheneth me. Philippians 4:13, KJV.

Therefore, in the present case I advise you: Leave these men alone! Let them go! For if their purpose or activity is of human origin, it will fail. But if it is from God, you will not be able to stop these men; you will only find yourselves fighting against God. Acts 5:38, 39, NIV.

Then I said, "I will not make mention of Him, Nor speak anymore in His name." But His word was in my heart like a burning fire Shut up in my bones; I was weary of holding it back, And I could not. Jeremiah 20:9, NKJV.

Then they called them in again and commanded them not to speak or teach at all in the name of Jesus. But Peter and John replied, "Which is right in God's eyes: to listen to you, or to him? You be the judges! As for us, we cannot help speaking about what we have seen and heard." Acts 4:18-20, NIV.

Let brotherly love continue. Do not forget to entertain strangers, for by so doing some have unwittingly entertained angels. Remember the prisoners as if chained with them—those who are mistreated—since you yourselves are in the body also. Hebrews 13:1–3, NKJV.

Let your light so shine before men, that they may see your good works and glorify your Father in heaven. Matthew 5:16, NKJV.

The Spirit of the Lord God is upon Me, Because the Lord has anointed Me To preach good tidings to the poor; He has sent Me to heal the brokenhearted, To proclaim liberty to the captives, And the opening of the prison to those who are bound; To proclaim the acceptable year of the Lord, And the day of vengeance of our God; To comfort all who mourn, To console those who mourn in Zion, To give them beauty for ashes, The oil of joy for mourning, The garment of praise for the spirit of heaviness; That they may be called trees of righteousness, The planting of the Lord, that He may be glorified. Isaiah 61:1–3, NKJV.

Chapter 11: Remember the Sabbath Day

Remember the Sabbath day, to keep it holy. Six days you shall labor and do all your work, but the seventh day is the Sabbath of the Lord your God. In it you shall do no work: you, nor your son, nor your daughter, nor your male servant, nor your female servant, nor your cattle, nor your stranger who is within your gates. For in six days the Lord made the heavens and the earth, the sea, and all that is in them, and rested the seventh day. Therefore the Lord blessed the Sabbath day and hallowed it. Exodus 20:8–11, NKJV.

And God said, Let there be light: and there was light. And God saw the light, that it was good: and God divided the light from the darkness.

And God called the light Day, and the darkness He called Night. And the evening and the morning were the first day. Genesis 1:3–5, KJV.

And on the seventh day God ended His work which He had done, and He rested on the seventh day from all His work which He had done. Then God blessed the seventh day and sanctified it, because in it He rested from all His work which God had created and made. Genesis 2:2, 3, NKJV.

The law of the Lord is perfect, converting the soul: the testimony of the Lord is sure, making wise the simple. The statutes of the Lord are right, rejoicing the heart: the commandment of the Lord is pure, enlightening the eyes. The fear of the Lord is clean, enduring for ever: the judgments of the Lord are true and righteous altogether. More to be desired are they than gold, yea, than much fine gold: sweeter also than honey and the honeycomb. Moreover by them is Thy servant warned: and in keeping of them there is great reward. Psalms 19:7–11, KJV.

Then the Lord said unto Moses, Behold, I will rain bread from heaven for you; and the people shall go out and gather a certain rate every day, that I may prove them, whether they will walk in My law, or no. And it shall come to pass, that on the sixth day they shall prepare that which they bring in; and it shall be twice as much as they gather daily. Exodus 16:4, 5, KJV.

And he said unto them, This is that which the LORD hath said, To morrow is the rest of the holy sabbath unto the LORD: bake that which ye will bake to day, and seethe that ye will seethe; and that which remaineth over lay up for you to be kept until the morning. Exodus 16:23, KJV.

If thou turn away thy foot from the Sabbath, from doing thy pleasure on My holy day; and call the Sabbath a delight, the holy of the Lord, honourable; and shalt honour Him, not doing thine own ways, nor finding thine own pleasure, nor speaking thine own words: Then shalt thou delight thyself in the Lord; and I will cause thee to ride upon the high places of the earth, and feed thee with the heritage of Jacob thy father: for the mouth of the Lord hath spoken it. Isaiah 58:13, 14, KJV.

And hallow My Sabbaths; and they shall be a sign between Me and you, that ye may know that I am the Lord your God. Ezekiel 20:20, KJV.

And He said unto them, "The Sabbath was made for man, and not man for the Sabbath: Therefore the Son of man is Lord also of the Sabbath." Mark 2:27, 28, KJV.

Moreover also I gave them My Sabbaths, to be a sign between Me and them, that they might know that I am the Lord that sanctify them. Ezekiel 20:12, KJV.

Think not that I am come to destroy the Law, or the Prophets: I am not come to destroy, but to fulfill. Matthew 5:17, KJV.

But pray ye that your flight be not in the winter, neither on the Sabbath day. Matthew 24:20, KJV.

And He came to Nazareth, where He had been brought up: and, as His custom was, He went into the synagogue on the Sabbath day, and stood up for to read. Luke 4:16, KJV.

So when the Jews went out of the synagogue, the Gentiles begged that these words might be preached to them the next Sabbath. Now when the congregation had broken up, many of the Jews and devout proselytes followed Paul and Barnabas, who, speaking to them, persuaded them to continue in the grace of God. On the next Sabbath almost the whole city came together to hear the word of God. Acts 13:42–44, NKJV.

Then Paul, as his custom was, went in to them, and for three Sabbaths reasoned with them from the Scriptures. Acts 17:2, NKJV.

And he reasoned in the synagogue every Sabbath, and persuaded the Jews and the Greeks. Acts 18:4, KJV.

My covenant will I not break, nor alter the thing that is gone out of My lips. Psalms 89:34, KJV.

For I am the Lord, I change not; therefore ye sons of Jacob are not consumed. Malachi 3:6, KJV.

And it is easier for heaven and earth to pass, than one tittle of the law to fail. Luke 16:17, KJV.

If ye love Me, keep My commandments. John 14:15, KJV.

By this we know that we love the children of God, when we love God, and keep His commandments. 1 John 5:2, KJV.

Here is the patience of the saints: here are they that keep the commandments of God, and the faith of Jesus. Revelation 14:12, KJV.

For as the new heavens and the new earth, which I will make, shall remain before Me, saith the Lord, so shall your seed and your name remain. And it shall come to pass, that from one new moon to another, and from one Sabbath to another, shall all flesh come to worship before Me, saith the Lord. Isaiah 66:22, 23, KJV.

Chapter 12: Flee Sexual Immorality

Flee sexual immorality. Every sin that a man does is outside the body, but he who commits sexual immorality sins against his own body. Or do you not know that your body is the temple of the Holy Spirit who is in you, whom you have from God, and you are not your own? For you were bought at a price; therefore glorify God in your body and in your spirit, which are God's. 1 Corinthians 6:18–20, NKJV.

As many as I love, I rebuke and chasten: be zealous therefore, and repent. Revelation 3:19, KJV.

Blessed is he whose transgression is forgiven, Whose sin is covered. Blessed is the man to whom the Lord does not impute iniquity, And in whose spirit there is no deceit. Psalms 32:1, 2, NKJV.

Therefore God also gave them up to uncleanness, in the lusts of their hearts, to dishonor their bodies among themselves, who exchanged the truth of God for the lie, and worshiped and served the creature rather than the Creator, who is blessed forever. Amen. For this reason God gave them up to vile passions. For even their women exchanged the natural use for what is against nature. Likewise also the men, leaving the natural use of the woman, burned in their lust for one another, men with men committing what is shameful, and receiving in themselves the penalty of their error which was due. And even as they did not like to retain God in their knowledge, God gave them over to a debased mind, to do those things which are not fitting; being filled with all unrighteousness, sexual immorality, wickedness, covetousness, maliciousness; full of envy, murder, strife, deceit, evil-mindedness; they are whisperers, backbiters, haters of God, violent, proud, boasters, inventors of evil things, disobedient to parents, undiscerning, untrustworthy, unloving, unforgiving, unmerciful; who, knowing the righteous judgment of God, that those who practice such things are deserving of death, not only do the same but also approve of those who practice them. Romans 1:24–32, NKJV.

Have mercy upon me, O God, according to thy lovingkindness: according unto the multitude of thy tender mercies blot out my transgressions. Wash me thoroughly from mine iniquity, and cleanse me from my sin. For I acknowledge my transgressions: and my sin is ever before me. Psalms 51:1–3, KJV.

He that covereth his sins shall not prosper: but whoso confesseth and forsaketh them shall have mercy. Proverbs 28:13, KJV.

He will again have compassion on us, And will subdue our iniquities. You will cast all our sins Into the depths of the sea. Micah 7:19, NKJV.

Dearly beloved, I beseech you as strangers and pilgrims, abstain from fleshly lusts, which war against the soul. 1 Peter 2:11, KJV.

The Lord appeared to us in the past, saying: "I have loved you with an everlasting love; I have drawn you with unfailing kindness." Jeremiah 31:3, NIV.

How can a young man cleanse his way? By taking heed according to Your word. With my whole heart I have sought You; Oh, let me not wander from Your commandments! Your word have I hidden in my heart, that I might not sin against You. Psalms 119:9-11, NKJV.

Search me, O God, and know my heart; Try me, and know my anxieties; And see if there is any wicked way in me, And lead me in the way everlasting. Psalms 139:23, 24, NKJV.

Do not be wise in your own eyes; Fear the Lord and depart from evil. It will be health to your flesh, And strength to your bones. Proverbs 3:7, 8, NKJV.

It is God's will that you should be sanctified: that you should avoid sexual immorality; that each of you should learn to control your own body in a way that is holy and honorable, not in passionate lust like the pagans, who do not know God; and that in this matter no one should wrong or take advantage of a brother or sister. The Lord will punish all those who commit such sins, as we told you and warned you before. For God did not call us to be impure, but to live a holy life. Therefore, anyone who rejects this instruction does not reject a human being but God, the very God who gives you His Holy Spirit. 1 Thessalonians 4:3–8, NIV.

For all have sinned, and come short of the glory of God; Being justified freely by His grace through the redemption that is in Christ Jesus. Romans 3:23, 24, KJV.

Seek the Lord while He may be found, Call upon Him while He is near. Let the wicked forsake his way, And the unrighteous man his thoughts; Let him return to the Lord, And He will have mercy on him; And to our God, For He will abundantly pardon. Isaiah 55:6, 7, NKJV.

If a man is righteous and does what is lawful and right—if he does not eat upon the mountains or lift up his eyes to the idols of the house of Israel, does not defile his neighbor's wife or approach a woman during her menstrual period. Ezekiel 18:5, 6, NRSV.

He who is faithful in what is least is faithful also in much; and he who is unjust in what is least is unjust also in much. Luke 16:10, NKJV.

Do not be deceived, God is not mocked; for whatever a man sows, that he will also reap. For he who sows to his flesh will of the flesh reap corruption, but he who sows to the Spirit will of the Spirit reap everlasting life. And let us not grow weary while doing good, for in due season we shall reap if we do not lose heart. Therefore, as we have opportunity, let us do good to all, especially to those who are of the household of faith. Galatians 6:7–10, NKJV.

For everything in the world—the lust of the flesh, the lust of the eyes, and the pride of life—comes not from the Father but from the world. The world and its desires pass away, but whoever does the will of God lives forever. 1 John 2:16, 17, NIV.

The acts of the flesh are obvious: sexual immorality, impurity and debauchery; idolatry and witchcraft; hatred, discord, jealousy, fits of rage, selfish ambition, dissensions, factions and envy; drunkenness, orgies, and the like. I warn you, as I did before, that those who live like this will not inherit the kingdom of God. Galatians 5:19–21, NIV.

Repent ye therefore, and be converted, that your sins may be blotted out, when the times of refreshing shall come from the presence of the Lord. Acts 3:19, KJV.

I, even I, am He that blotteth out thy transgressions for Mine own sake, and will not remember thy sins. Isaiah 43:25, KJV.

If we say that we have no sin, we deceive ourselves, and the truth is not in us. If we confess our sins, He is faithful and just to forgive us our sins and to cleanse us from all unrighteousness. 1 John 1:8, 9, NKJV.

But God proves His love for us in that while we were still sinners Christ died for us. Romans 5:8, NRSV.

Who desires everyone to be saved and to come to the knowledge of the truth. 1 Timothy 2:4, NRSV.

Receive my instruction, and not silver; and knowledge rather than choice gold. For wisdom is better than rubies; and all the things that may be desired are not to be compared to it. Proverbs 8:10, 11, KJV.

If any of you lacks wisdom, you should ask God, who gives generously to all without finding fault, and it will be given to you. James 1:5, NIV.

Your ears shall hear a word behind you, saying, "This is the way, walk in it," Whenever you turn to the right hand Or whenever you turn to the left. Isaiah 30:21, NKJV.

And I will cleanse them from all their iniquity, whereby they have sinned against Me; and I will pardon all their iniquities, whereby they have sinned, and whereby they have transgressed against Me. Jeremiah 33:8, KJV.

Jerusalem, wash the evil from your heart and be saved. How long will you harbor wicked thoughts? Jeremiah 4:14, NIV.

I delight to do Your will, Oh my God, And Your law is within my heart. Psalms 40:8, NKJV.

Those who are victorious will inherit all this, and I will be their God and they will be My children. But the cowardly, the unbelieving, the vile, the murderers, the sexually immoral, those who practice magic arts, the idolaters and all liars—they will be consigned to the fiery lake of burning sulfur. This is the second death. Revelation 21:7, 8, NIV.

Therefore let him who thinks he stands take heed lest he fall. No temptation has overtaken you except such as is common to man; but God is faithful, who will not allow you to be tempted beyond what you are able, but with the temptation will also make the way of escape, that you may be able to bear it. 1 Corinthians 10:12, 13, NKJV.

… Behold, the fear of the Lord, that is wisdom, And to depart from evil is understanding. Job 28:28, NKJV.

But as for you, man of God, shun all this; pursue righteousness, godliness, faith, love, endurance, gentleness. Fight the good fight of the faith; take hold of the eternal life, to which you were called and for which you made the good confession in the presence of many witnesses. 1 Timothy 6:11, 12, NRSV.

For I know the thoughts that I think toward you, says the Lord, thoughts of peace and not of evil, to give you a future and a hope. Then you will call upon Me and go and pray to Me, and I will listen to you. And you will seek Me and find Me, when you search for Me with all your heart. Jeremiah 29:11-13, NKJV.

Do you not know that you are the temple of God and that the Spirit of God dwells in you? If anyone defiles the temple of God, God will destroy him. For the temple of God is holy, which temple you are. 1 Corinthians 3:16, 17, NKJV.

Blessed are those who do His commandments, that they may have the right to the tree of life, and may enter through the gates into the city.

But outside are dogs and sorcerers and sexually immoral and murderers and idolaters, and whoever loves and practices a lie. "I, Jesus, have sent My angel to testify to you these things in the churches. I am the Root and the Offspring of David, the Bright and Morning Star." And the Spirit and the bride say, "Come!" And let him who hears say, "Come!" And let him who thirsts come. Whoever desires, let him take the water of life freely. Revelation 22:14–17, NKJV.

Brethren, if anyone among you wanders from the truth, and someone turns him back, let him know that he who turns a sinner from the error of his way will save a soul from death and cover a multitude of sins. James 5:19, 20, NKJV.

It is actually reported that there is sexual immorality among you, and of a kind that even pagans do not tolerate: A man is sleeping with his father's wife. 1 Corinthians 5:1, NIV.

I wrote to you in my letter not to associate with sexually immoral people—not at all meaning the people of this world who are immoral, or the greedy and swindlers, or idolaters. In that case you would have to leave this world. But now I am writing to you that you must not associate with anyone who claims to be a brother or sister but is sexually immoral or greedy, an idolater or slanderer, a drunkard or swindler. Do not even eat with such people. What business is it of mine to judge those outside the church? Are you not to judge those inside? God will judge those outside. "Expel the wicked person from among you." 1 Corinthians 5:9–13, NIV.

Oh Lord, correct me, but with justice; Not in Your anger, lest You bring me to nothing. Jeremiah 10:24, NKJV.

Whoever walks blamelessly will be saved, But he who is perverse in his ways will suddenly fall. Proverbs 28:18, NKJV.

When they kept on questioning Him, He straightened up and said to them, "Let any one of you who is without sin be the first to throw a stone at her." ... "Then neither do I condemn you," Jesus declared. "Go now and leave your life of sin." John 8:7, 11, NIV.

Brethren, if a man is overtaken in any trespass, you who are spiritual restore such a one in a spirit of gentleness, considering yourself lest you also be tempted. Bear one another's burdens, and so fulfill the law of Christ. Galatians 6:1, 2, NKJV.

I will instruct you and teach you in the way you should go; I will guide you with My eye. Psalms 32:8, NKJV.

Finally, brethren, whatever things are true, whatever things are noble, whatever things are just, whatever things are pure, whatever things are lovely, whatever things are of good report, if there is any virtue and if there is anything praiseworthy—meditate on these things. The things which you learned and received and heard and saw in me, these do, and the God of peace will be with you. Philippians 4:8, 9, NKJV.

Create in me a pure heart, O God, and renew a steadfast spirit within me. Do not cast me from Your presence or take Your Holy Spirit from me. Restore to me the joy of Your salvation and grant me a willing spirit, to sustain me. Then I will teach transgressors Your ways, so that sinners will turn back to You. Psalms 51:10–13, NIV.

Chapter 13: Forgive, and You Will Be Forgiven

Judge not, and you shall not be judged. Condemn not, and you shall not be condemned. Forgive, and you will be forgiven. Luke 6:37, NKJV.

Therefore, as God's chosen people, holy and dearly loved, clothe yourselves with compassion, kindness, humility, gentleness and patience. Bear with each other and forgive one another if any of you has a grievance against someone. Forgive as the Lord forgave you. And over all these virtues put on love, which binds them all together in perfect unity. Let the peace of Christ rule in your hearts, since as members of one body you were called to peace. And be thankful. Colossians 3:12-15, NIV.

And whenever you stand praying, if you have anything against anyone, forgive him, that your Father in heaven may also forgive you your trespasses. But if you do not forgive, neither will your Father in heaven forgive your trespasses. Mark 11:25, 26, NKJV.

Then came Peter to Him, and said, Lord, how oft shall my brother sin against me, and I forgive him? till seven times?" Jesus saith unto him, I say not unto thee, Until seven times: but, Until seventy times seven. Matthew 18:21, 22, KJV.

Be ye angry, and sin not: let not the sun go down upon your wrath: Neither give place to the devil. Let all bitterness, and wrath, and anger, and clamour, and evil speaking, be put away from you, with all malice: And be ye kind one to another, tenderhearted, forgiving one another, even as God for Christ's sake hath forgiven you. Ephesians 4:26, 27, 31, 32, KJV.

Blessed is he whose transgression is forgiven, Whose sin is covered. Blessed is the man to whom the Lord does not impute iniquity, And in whose spirit there is no deceit. Psalms 32:1, 2, NKJV.

When they came to the place called the Skull, they crucified Him there, along with the criminals—one on His right, the other on His left. Jesus said, "Father, forgive them, for they do not know what they are doing." And they divided up His clothes by casting lots. Luke 23:33, 34, NIV.

But I say to you who hear: Love your enemies, do good to those who hate you, bless those who curse you, and pray for those who spitefully use you. Luke 6:27, 28, NKJV.

Do not speak evil against one another, brothers and sisters. Whoever speaks evil against another or judges another, speaks evil against the law and judges the law; but if you judge the law, you are not a doer of the law but a judge. There is one Lawgiver and judge who is able to save and to destroy. So who, then, are you to judge your neighbor? James 4:11, 12, NRSV.

Do not judge, so that you may not be judged. For with the judgement you make you will be judged, and the measure you give will be the measure you get. Why do you see the speck in your neighbor's eye, but do not notice the log in your own eye? Or how can you say to your neighbor, "Let me take the speck out of your eye," while the log is in your own eye? You hypocrite, first take the log out of your own eye, and then you will see clearly to take the speck out of your neighbor's eye. Matthew 7:1–5, NRSV.

For God so loved the world, that He gave His only begotten Son, that whosoever believeth in Him should not perish, but have everlasting life. For God sent not His Son into the world to condemn the world; but that the world through Him might be saved. John 3:16, 17, KJV.

I, even I, am He that blotteth out thy transgressions for Mine own sake, and will not remember thy sins. Isaiah 43:25, KJV.

Have mercy upon me, O God, according to thy lovingkindness: according unto the multitude of thy tender mercies blot out my transgressions. Wash me thoroughly from mine iniquity, and cleanse me from my sin. For I acknowledge my transgressions: and my sin is ever before me. Psalms 51:1–3, KJV.

But if the wicked will turn from all his sins that he hath committed, and keep all My statutes, and do that which is lawful and right, he shall surely live, he shall not die. All his transgressions that he hath committed, they shall not be mentioned unto him: in his righteousness that he hath done he shall live. Have I any pleasure at all that the wicked should die? saith the Lord God: and not that he should return from his ways, and live? Ezekiel 18:21–23, KJV.

I say unto you, that likewise joy shall be in heaven over one sinner that repenteth, more than over ninety and nine just persons, which need no repentance. Likewise, I say unto you, there is joy in the presence of the angels of God over one sinner that repenteth. Luke 15:7, 10, KJV.

Then I acknowledged my sin to You and did not cover up my iniquity. I said, "I will confess my transgressions to the Lord." And You forgave the guilt of my sin. Psalms 32:5, NIV.

And I will cleanse them from all their iniquity, whereby they have sinned against Me; and I will pardon all their iniquities, whereby they have sinned, and whereby they have transgressed against Me. Jeremiah 33:8, KJV.

For all have sinned, and come short of the glory of God; Being justified freely by His grace through the redemption that is in Christ Jesus. Romans 3:23, 24, KJV.

Who are you to judge someone else's servant? To their own master, servants stand or fall. And they will stand, for the Lord is able to make them stand. You, then, why do you judge your brother or sister? Or why do you treat them with contempt? For we will all stand before God's judgement seat. It is written: "As surely as I live," says the Lord, "every knee will bow before Me; every tongue will acknowledge God." So then, each of us will give an account of ourselves to God. Therefore let us stop passing judgement on one another. Instead, make up your mind not to put any stumbling block or obstacle in the way of a brother or sister. Romans 14:4, 10–13, NIV.

But with me it is a very small thing that I should be judged by you or by a human court. In fact, I do not even judge myself. For I know of nothing against myself, yet I am not justified by this; but He who judges me is the Lord. Therefore judge nothing before the time, until the Lord comes, who will both bring to light the hidden things of darkness and reveal the counsels of the hearts. Then each one's praise will come from God. 1 Corinthians 4:3–5, NKJV.

If we say that we have no sin, we deceive ourselves, and the truth is not in us. If we confess our sins, He is faithful and just to forgive us our sins and to cleanse us from all unrighteousness. 1 John 1:8, 9, NKJV.

He hath not dealt with us after our sins; nor rewarded us according to our iniquities. For as the heaven is high above the earth, so great is His mercy toward them that fear Him. As far as the east is from the west, so far hath He removed our transgressions from us. Like as a father pitieth his children, so the Lord pitieth them that fear Him. For He knoweth our frame; He remembereth that we are dust. Psalms 103:10–14, KJV.

The Lord is longsuffering, and of great mercy, forgiving iniquity and transgression, and by no means clearing the guilty, visiting the iniquity of the fathers upon the children unto the third and fourth generation. Numbers 14:18, KJV.

Let the wicked forsake his way, And the unrighteous man his thoughts; Let him return to the Lord, And He will have mercy on him; And to our God, For He will abundantly pardon. Isaiah 55:7, NKJV.

There was a certain creditor which had two debtors: the one owed five hundred pence, and the other fifty. And when they had nothing to pay, he frankly forgave them both. Tell Me therefore, which of them will love him most? Wherefore I say unto thee, Her sins, which are many, are forgiven; for she loved much: but to whom little is forgiven, the same loveth little. Luke 7:41, 42, 47, KJV.

For if ye forgive men their trespasses, your heavenly Father will also forgive you: But if ye forgive not men their trespasses, neither will your Father forgive your trespasses. Matthew 6:14, 15, KJV.

Repent ye therefore, and be converted, that your sins may be blotted out, when the times of refreshing shall come from the presence of the Lord. Acts 3:19, KJV.

Chapter 14: Is Anyone Among You Sick?

Is anyone among you suffering? Let him pray. Is anyone cheerful? Let him sing Psalms. Is anyone among you sick? Let him call for the elders of the church, and let them pray over him, anointing him with oil in the name of the Lord. And the prayer of faith will save the sick, and the Lord will raise him up. And if he has committed sins, he will be forgiven. Confess your trespasses to one another, and pray for one another, that you may be healed. The effective, fervent prayer of a righteous man avails much. Elijah was a man with a nature like ours, and he prayed earnestly that it would not rain; and it did not rain on the land for three years and six months. And he prayed again, and the heaven gave rain, and the earth produced its fruit. James 5:13–18, NKJV.

He healeth the broken in heart, and bindeth up their wounds. Psalms 147:3, KJV.

And, behold, a woman, which was diseased with an issue of blood twelve years, came behind Him, and touched the hem of His garment: For she said within herself, If I may but touch His garment, I shall be whole. But Jesus turned Him about, and when He saw her, He said, Daughter, be of good comfort; thy faith hath made thee whole. And the woman was made whole from that hour. Matthew 9:20–22, KJV.

When He entered Capernaum, a centurion came to Him, appealing to Him and saying, "Lord, my servant is lying at home paralyzed, in terrible distress." And He said to him, "I will come and cure him." The centurion answered, "Lord, I am not worthy to have You come under my roof; but only speak the word, and my servant will be healed. For I also am a man under authority, with soldiers under me; and I say to one, "Go,' and he goes, and to another, "Come,' and he comes, and to my slave, "Do this,' and the slave does it." When Jesus heard him, He was amazed and said to those who followed Him, "Truly I tell you, in no one in Israel have I found such faith. I tell you, many will come from east and west and will eat with Abraham and Isaac and Jacob in the kingdom of heaven, while the heirs of the kingdom will be thrown into the outer darkness, where there will be weeping and gnashing of teeth." And to the centurion Jesus said, "Go; let it be done for you according to your faith." And the servant was healed in that hour. Matthew 8:5–13, NRSV.

And, behold, two blind men sitting by the way side, when they heard that Jesus passed by, cried out, saying, Have mercy on us, O Lord, thou Son of David. And the multitude rebuked them, because they should hold their peace: but they cried the more, saying, Have mercy on us, O Lord, thou Son of David. And Jesus stood still, and called them, and said, What will ye that I shall do unto you? They said unto Him, Lord, that our eyes may be opened. So Jesus had compassion on them, and touched their eyes: and immediately their eyes received sight, and they followed Him. Matthew 20:30–34, KJV.

Just then there was in their synagogue a man with an unclean spirit, and he cried out, "What have You to do with us, Jesus of Nazareth? Have You come to destroy us? I know who You are, the Holy One of God." But Jesus rebuked him, saying, "Be silent, and come out of him!" And the unclean spirit, convulsing him and crying with a loud voice, came out of him. They were all amazed, and they kept on asking one another, "What is this? A new teaching—with authority! He commands even the unclean spirits, and they obey Him." At once His fame began to spread throughout the surrounding region of Galilee. As soon as they left the synagogue, they entered the house of Simon and Andrew, with James and John. Now Simon's mother-in-law was in bed with a fever, and they told Him about her at once. He came and took her by the hand and lifted her up. Then the fever left her, and she began to serve them. That evening, at sundown, they brought to Him all who were sick or possessed with demons. And the whole city was gathered around the door. And He cured many who were sick with various diseases, and cast out many demons; and He would not permit the demons to speak, because they knew Him. Mark 1:23–34, NRSV.

A leper came to Him begging Him, and kneeling he said to Him, "If You choose, You can make me clean." Moved with pity, Jesus stretched out His hand and touched him, and said to him, "I do choose. Be made clean!" Immediately the leprosy left him, and he was made clean. Mark 1:40–42, NRSV.

In these lay a great multitude of sick people, blind, lame, paralyzed, waiting for the moving of the water. For an angel went down at a certain time into the pool and stirred up the water; then whoever stepped in first, after the stirring of the water, was made well of whatever disease he had. Now a certain man was there who had an infirmity thirty-eight years. When Jesus saw him lying there, and knew that he already had been in that condition a long time, He said to him, "Do you want to be made well?" The sick man answered Him, "Sir, I have no man to put me into the pool when the water is stirred up; but while I am coming, another steps down before me." Jesus said to him, "Rise, take up your bed and walk." And immediately the man was made well, took up his bed, and walked. And that day was the Sabbath. John 5:3–9, NKJV.

Peter sent them all out of the room; then he got down on his knees and prayed. Turning to the dead woman, he said, "Tabitha, get up." She opened her eyes, and seeing Peter she sat up. Acts 9:40, NIV.

Bless the Lord, O my soul: and all that is within me, bless His holy name. Bless the Lord, O my soul, and forget not all His benefits: Who forgiveth all thine iniquities; who healeth all thy diseases; Who redeemeth thy life from destruction; who crowneth thee with lovingkindness and tender mercies; Who satisfieth thy mouth with good things; so that thy youth is renewed like the eagle's. Psalms 103:1–5, KJV.

Chapter 15: The Dead Know Nothing

For the living know that they will die; But the dead know nothing, And they have no more reward, For the memory of them is forgotten. Also their love, their hatred, and their envy have now perished; Nevermore will they have a share In anything done under the sun. Ecclesiastes 9:5, 6, NKJV.

And the Lord God formed man of the dust of the ground, and breathed into his nostrils the breath of life; and man became a living being. Genesis 2:7, NKJV.

In the sweat of thy face shalt thou eat bread, till thou return unto the ground; for out of it wast thou taken: for dust thou art, and unto dust shalt thou return. Genesis 3:19, KJV.

Then shall the dust return to the earth as it was: and the spirit shall return unto God who gave it. Ecclesiastes 12:7, KJV.

As the cloud disappears and vanishes away, So he who goes down to the grave does not come up. He shall never return to his house, Nor shall his place know him anymore. Job 7:9, 10, NKJV.

These things He said, and after that He said to them, "Our friend Lazarus sleeps, but I go that I may wake him up." Then His disciples said, "Lord, if he sleeps he will get well." However, Jesus spoke of his death, but they thought that He was speaking about taking rest in sleep. Then Jesus said to them plainly, "Lazarus is dead." … Martha said to Him, "I know that he will rise again in the resurrection at the last day." Jesus said to her, "I am the resurrection and the life. He who believes in Me, though he may die, he shall live. And whoever lives and believes in Me shall never die. Do you believe this?" She said to Him, "Yes, Lord, I believe that You are the Christ, the Son of God, who is come into the world." John 11:11–14, 24–27, NKJV.

At that moment the curtain of the temple was torn in two from top to bottom. The earth shook, the rocks split and the tombs broke open. The bodies of many holy people who had died were raised to life. They came out of the tombs after Jesus' resurrection and went into the holy city and appeared to many people. Matthew 27:51–53, NIV.

Jesus saith unto her, Touch me not; for I am not yet ascended to My Father: but go to My brethren, and say unto them, I ascend unto My Father, and your Father; and to My God, and your God. John 20:17, KJV.

The dead praise not the Lord, neither any that go down into silence. Psalms 115:17, KJV.

You hide Your face, they are troubled; You take away their breath, they die and return to their dust. Psalms 104:29, NKJV.

Do not put your trust in princes, in mortals, in whom there is no help. When their breath departs, they return to the earth; on that very day their plans perish. Psalms 146:3, 4, NRSV.

But I do not want you to be ignorant, brethren, concerning those who have fallen asleep, lest you sorrow as others who have no hope. For if we believe that Jesus died and rose again, even so God will bring with Him those who sleep in Jesus. For this we say to you by the word of the Lord, that we who are alive and remain until the coming of the Lord will by no means precede those who are asleep. For the Lord Himself will descend from heaven with a shout, with the voice of an archangel, and with the trumpet of God. And the dead in Christ will rise first. Then we who are alive and remain shall be caught up together with them in the clouds to meet the Lord in the air. And thus we shall always be with the Lord. Therefore comfort one another with these words. 1 Thessalonians 4:13–18, NKJV.

Men and brethren, let me speak freely unto you of the patriarch David, that he is both dead and buried, and his sepulcher is with us unto this day. Acts 2:29, KJV.

For the wages of sin is death; but the gift of God is eternal life through Jesus Christ our Lord. Romans 6:23, KJV.

Now this I say, brethren, that flesh and blood cannot inherit the kingdom of God; neither doth corruption inherit incorruption. Behold, I shew you a mystery; We shall not all sleep, but we shall all be changed, In a moment, in the twinkling of an eye, at the last trump: for the trumpet shall sound, and the dead shall be raised incorruptible, and we shall be changed. For this corruptible must put on incorruption, and this mortal must put on immortality. So when this corruptible shall have put on incorruption, and this mortal shall have put on immortality, then shall be brought to pass the saying that is written, Death is swallowed up in victory. O Death, where is thy sting? O Grave, where is thy victory? The sting of death is sin; and the strength of sin is the law. But thanks be to God, which giveth us the victory through our Lord Jesus Christ. Therefore, my beloved brethren, be ye steadfast, unmovable, always abounding in the work of the Lord, forasmuch as ye know that your labour is not in vain in the Lord. 1 Corinthians 15:50–58, KJV.

Then I heard a voice from heaven say, "Write this: Blessed are the dead who die in the Lord from now on." "Yes," says the Spirit, "they will rest from their labor, for their deeds will follow them." Revelation 14:13, NIV.

And this is the will of Him that sent Me, that every one which seeth the Son, and believeth on Him, may have everlasting life: and I will raise him up at the last day. John 6:40, KJV.

Chapter 16: You Will Have Tribulation

Most assuredly, I say to you that you will weep and lament, but the world will rejoice; and you will be sorrowful, but your sorrow will be turned into joy. These things I have spoken to you, that in Me you may have peace. In the world you will have tribulation; but be of good cheer, I have overcome the world. John 16:20, 33, NKJV.

And who is he who will harm you if you become followers of what is good? But even if you should suffer for righteousness' sake, you are blessed. "And do not be afraid of their threats, nor be troubled." But sanctify the Lord God in your hearts, and always be ready to give a defense to everyone who asks you a reason for the hope that is in you, with meekness and fear; having a good conscience, that when they defame you as evildoers, those who revile your good conduct in Christ may be ashamed. For it is better, if it is the will of God, to suffer for doing good than for doing evil. 1 Peter 3:13–17, NKJV.

But you are a chosen generation, a royal priesthood, a holy nation, His own special people, that you may proclaim the praises of Him who called you out of darkness into His marvelous light: who once were not a people but are now the people of God, who had not obtained mercy but now have obtained mercy. 1 Peter 2:9, 10, NKJV.

Beloved, do not think it strange concerning the fiery trial which is to try you, as though some strange thing happened to you; but rejoice to the extent that you partake of Christ's sufferings, that when His glory is revealed, you may also be glad with exceeding joy. If you are reproached for the name of Christ, blessed are you, for the Spirit of glory and of God rests upon you. On their part He is blasphemed, but on your part He is glorified. 1 Peter 4:12–14, NKJV.

My brethren, count it all joy when you fall into various trials, knowing that the testing of your faith produces patience. But let patience have its perfect work, that you may be perfect and complete, lacking nothing. James 1:2–4, NKJV.

Blessed be God, even the Father of our Lord Jesus Christ, the Father of mercies, and the God of all comfort; Who comforteth us in all our tribulation, that we may be able to comfort them which are in any trouble, by the comfort wherewith we ourselves are comforted of God. 2 Corinthians 1:3, 4, KJV.

Blessed are the poor in spirit, For theirs is the kingdom of heaven. Blessed are those who mourn, For they shall be comforted. Blessed are the meek, For they shall inherit the earth. Blessed are those who hunger and thirst for righteousness, For they shall be filled. Blessed are the merciful, For they shall obtain mercy. Blessed are the pure in heart, For they shall see God. Blessed are the peacemakers, For they shall be called sons of God. Blessed are those who are persecuted for righteousness' sake, For theirs is the kingdom of heaven. Blessed are you when they revile and persecute you, and say all kinds of evil against you falsely for My sake. Rejoice and be exceedingly glad, for great is your reward in heaven, for so they persecuted the prophets who were before you. Matthew 5:3–12, NKJV.

They will take up serpents; and if they drink anything deadly, it will by no means hurt them; they will lay hands on the sick, and they will recover. Mark 16:18, NKJV.

When you pass through the waters, I will be with you; And through the rivers, they shall not overflow you. When you walk through the fire, you shall not be burned, Nor shall the flame scorch you. Isaiah 43:2, NKJV.

For in the time of trouble He shall hide me in His pavilion; In the secret place of His tabernacle He shall hide me; He shall set me high upon a rock. Psalms 27:5, NKJV.

For I reckon that the sufferings of this present time are not worthy to be compared with the glory which shall be revealed in us. And we know that all things work together for good to them that love God, to them who are the called according to His purpose. Romans 8:18, 28, KJV.

You are my hiding place; you will protect me from trouble and surround me with songs of deliverance. Psalms 32:7, NIV.

Then the dragon was angry with the woman, and went off to make war on the rest of her children, those who keep the commandments of God and hold the testimony of Jesus. Revelation 12:17, NRSV.

Now the Spirit expressly says that in latter times some will renounce the faith by paying attention to deceitful spirits and teachings of demons, through the hypocrisy of liars whose consciences are seared with a hot iron. They forbid marriage and demand abstinence from foods, which God created to be received with thanksgiving by those who believe and know the truth. 1 Timothy 4:1–3, NRSV.

On My account you will be brought before governors and kings as witnesses to them and to the Gentiles. But when they arrest you, do not worry about what to say or how to say it. At that time you will be given what to say, for it will not be you speaking, but the Spirit of your Father speaking through you. Matthew 10:18–20, NIV.

Servants, be submissive to your masters with all fear, not only to the good and gentle, but also to the harsh. For this is commendable, if because of conscience toward God one endures grief, suffering wrongfully. For what credit is it if, when you are beaten for your faults, you take it patiently? But when you do good and suffer, if you take it patiently, this is commendable before God. For to this you were called, because Christ also suffered for us, leaving us an example, that you should follow His steps. 1 Peter 2:18–21, NKJV.

Indeed, all who want to live a godly life in Christ Jesus will be persecuted. But wicked people and imposters will go from bad to worse, deceiving others and being deceived. But as for you, continue in what you have learned and firmly believed, knowing from whom you learned it, and how from childhood you have known the sacred writings that are able to instruct you for salvation through faith in Christ Jesus. 2 Timothy 3:12–15, NRSV.

I, even I, am he who comforts you. Who are you that you fear mere mortals, human beings who are but grass? Isaiah 51:12, NIV.

For whosoever will save his life shall lose it; but whosoever shall lose his life for My sake and the gospel's, the same shall save it. For what shall it profit a man, if he shall gain the whole world, and lose his own soul? Or what shall a man give in exchange for his soul? Whosoever therefore shall be ashamed of Me and of My words in this adulterous and sinful generation; of him also shall the Son of Man be ashamed, when He cometh in the glory of His Father with the holy angels. Mark 8:35–38, KJV.

The Lord also will be a refuge for the oppressed, a refuge in times of trouble. And they that know Thy name will put their trust in Thee: for Thou, Lord, hast not forsaken them that seek Thee. Psalms 9:9, 10, KJV.

But I say to you, Love your enemies and pray for those who persecute you. Matthew 5:44, NRSV.

From there you will seek the Lord your God, and you will find Him if you search after Him with all your heart and soul. In your distress, when all these things have happened to you in time to come, you will return to the Lord your God and heed Him. Because the Lord your God is a merciful God, He will neither abandon you nor destroy you; He will not forget the covenant with your ancestors that He swore to them. Deuteronomy 4:29–31, NRSV.

God is our refuge and strength, an ever-present help in trouble. Therefore we will not fear, though the earth give way and the mountains fall into the heart of the sea, though its waters roar and foam and the mountains quake with their surging. Psalms 46:1–3, NIV.

… This is what the Lord says to you: "Do not be afraid or discouraged because of this vast army. For the battle is not yours, but God's. You will not have to fight this battle. Take up your positions; stand firm and see the deliverance the Lord will give you, Judah and Jerusalem. Do not be afraid; do not be discouraged. Go out to face them tomorrow, and the Lord will be with you." When the men of Judah came to the place that overlooks the desert and looked toward the vast army, they saw only dead bodies lying on the ground; no one had escaped. 2 Chronicles 20:15, 17, 24, NIV.

For many shall come in My name, saying, I am Christ; and shall deceive many. And ye shall hear of wars and rumors of wars: see that ye be not troubled: for all these things must come to pass, but the end is not yet. For nation shall rise against nation, and kingdom against kingdom: and there shall be famines, and pestilences, and earthquakes, in divers places. All these are the beginning of sorrows. Then shall they deliver you up to be afflicted, and shall kill you: and ye shall be hated of all nations for My name's sake. And then shall many be offended, and shall betray one another, and shall hate one another. And many false prophets shall rise, and shall deceive many. And because iniquity shall abound, the love of many shall wax cold. But he that shall endure unto the end, the same shall be saved. And this gospel of the kingdom shall be preached in all the world for a witness unto all nations; and then shall the end come. Matthew 24:5–14, KJV.

For they are spirits of devils, working miracles, which go forth unto the kings of the earth and of the whole world, to gather them to the battle of that great day of God Almighty. Revelation 16:14, KJV.

For then shall be great tribulation, such as was not since the beginning of the world to this time, no, nor ever shall be. And except those days should be shortened, there should no flesh be saved: but for the elect's sake those days shall be shortened. Then if any man shall say unto you, Lo, here is Christ, or there; believe it not. For there shall arise false Christs, and false prophets, and shall shew great signs and wonders; insomuch that, if it were possible, they shall deceive the very elect. Behold, I have told you before. Wherefore if they shall say unto you, Behold, He is in the desert; go not forth: behold, he is in the secret chambers; believe it not. For as the lightning cometh out of the east, and shineth even unto the west; so shall also the coming of the Son of Man be. Matthew 24:21–27, KJV.

And except that the Lord had shortened those days, no flesh should be saved: but for the elect's sake, whom He hath chosen, He hath shortened the days. Mark 13:20, KJV.

And now I have told you before it come to pass, that, when it is come to pass, ye might believe. John 14:29, KJV.

For this reason I also suffer these things; nevertheless I am not ashamed, for I know whom I have believed and am persuaded that He is able to keep what I have committed to Him until that Day. 2 Timothy 1:12, NKJV.

I have fought the good fight, I have finished the race, I have kept the faith. Finally, there is laid up for me the crown of righteousness, which the Lord, the righteous Judge, will give to me on that Day, and not to me only but also to all who have loved His appearing. 2 Timothy 4:7, 8, NKJV.

Chapter 17: Fear Not for I Am with You

Fear not, for I am with you; Be not dismayed, for I am your God. I will strengthen you, Yes, I will help you, I will uphold you with My righteous right hand. Isaiah 41:10, NKJV.

Therefore I say to you, do not worry about your life, what you will eat or what you will drink; nor about your body, what you will put on. Is not life more than food and the body more than clothing? Look at the birds of the air, for they neither sow nor reap nor gather into barns; yet your heavenly Father feeds them. Are you not of more value than they? Which of you by worrying can add one cubit to his stature? So why do you worry about clothing? Consider the lilies of the field, how they grow: they neither toil nor spin; and yet I say to you that even Solomon in all his glory was not arrayed like one of these. Now if God so clothes the grass of the field, which today is, and tomorrow is thrown into the oven, will He not much more clothe you, O you of little faith? Therefore do not worry, saying, "What shall we eat?" or "What shall we drink?" or "What shall we wear?" For after all these things the Gentiles seek. For your heavenly Father knows that you need all these things. But seek first the kingdom of God and His righteousness, and all these things shall be added to you. Therefore do not worry about tomorrow, for tomorrow will worry about its own things. Sufficient for the day is its own trouble. Matthew 6:25–34, NKJV.

You will keep him in perfect peace, Whose mind is stayed on You, Because he trusts in You. Isaiah 26:3, NKJV.

As for me, I am poor and needy, but the Lord takes thought of me. You are my help and my deliverer; do not delay, O my God. Psalms 40:17, NRSV.

Wait on the Lord: be of good courage, and He shall strengthen thine heart: wait, I say, on the Lord. Psalms 27:14, KJV.

Sing, O heavens; and be joyful, O earth; and break forth into singing, O mountains: for the Lord hath comforted His people, and will have mercy upon His afflicted. Isaiah 49:13, KJV.

Blessed are ye that hunger now: for ye shall be filled. Blessed are ye that weep now: for ye shall laugh. Luke 6:21, KJV.

And we have known and believed the love that God hath to us. God is love; and he that dwelleth in love dwelleth in God, and God in him. Herein is our love made perfect, that we may have boldness in the day of judgment: because as He is, so are we in this world. There is no fear in love; but perfect love casteth out fear: because fear hath torment. He that feareth is not made perfect in love. We love Him, because He first loved us. 1 John 4:16–19, KJV.

The Lord bless thee, and keep thee: The Lord make His face shine upon thee, and be gracious unto thee: The Lord lift up His countenance upon thee, and give thee peace. Numbers 6:24–26, KJV.

Peace I leave with you; my peace I give you. I do not give to you as the world gives. Do not let your hearts be troubled and do not be afraid. John 14:27, NIV.

Be anxious for nothing, but in everything by prayer and supplication, with thanksgiving, let your requests be made known to God; and the peace of God, which surpasses all understanding, will guard your hearts and minds through Christ Jesus. Philippians 4:6, 7, NKJV.

Are not five sparrows sold for two pennies? Yet not one of them is forgotten by God. Indeed, the very hairs of your head are all numbered. Don't be afraid; you are worth more than many sparrows. And do not set your heart on what you will eat or drink; do not worry about it. For the pagan world runs after all such things, and your Father knows that you need them. But seek His kingdom, and these things will be given to you as well. Luke 12:6, 7, 29–31, NIV.

He will cover you with his feathers, and under his wings you will find refuge; his faithfulness will be your shield and rampart. You will not fear the terror of night, nor the arrow that flies by day, nor the pestilence that stalks in the darkness, nor the plague that destroys at midday, Psalms 91:4-6, NIV.

I will both lie down in peace, and sleep; For You alone, O Lord, make me dwell in safety. Psalms 4:8, NKJV.

The Lord is my light and my salvation; whom shall I fear? the Lord is the strength of my life; of whom shall I be afraid? Psalms 27:1, KJV.

The Lord is my shepherd; I shall not want. He maketh me to lie down in green pastures: He leadeth me beside the still waters. He restoreth my soul: He leadeth me in the paths of righteousness for His name's sake. Yea, though I walk through the valley of the shadow of death, I will fear no evil: for Thou art with me; Thy rod and Thy staff they comfort me. Thou preparest a table before me in the presence of mine enemies: Thou anointest my head with oil; my cup runneth over. Surely goodness and mercy shall follow me all the days of my life: and I will dwell in the house of the Lord for ever. Psalms 23, KJV.

When thou liest down, thou shalt not be afraid: yea, thou shalt lie down, and thy sleep shall be sweet. Be not afraid of sudden fear, neither of the desolation of the wicked, when it cometh. For the Lord shall be thy confidence, and shall keep thy foot from being taken. Proverbs 3:24–26, KJV.

But blessed is the one who trusts in the Lord, whose confidence is in Him. They will be like a tree planted by the water that sends out its roots by the stream. It does not fear when heat comes; its leaves are always green. It has no worries in a year of drought and never fails to bear fruit. Jeremiah 17:7, 8, NIV.

For God did not give us a spirit of cowardice, but rather a spirit of power and of love and of self-discipline. 2 Timothy 1:7, NRSV.

The waves of death swirled about me; the torrents of destruction overwhelmed me. The cords of the grave coiled around me; the snares of death confronted me. In my distress I called to the Lord; I called out to my God. From His temple he heard my voice; my cry came to His ears. 2 Samuel 22:5–7, NIV.

I was young and now I am old, yet I have never seen the righteous forsaken or their children begging bread. Psalms 37:25, NIV.

Humble yourselves, therefore, under God's mighty hand, that He may lift you up in due time. Cast all your anxiety on Him because He cares for you. 1 Peter 5:6, 7, NIV.

Have I not commanded thee? Be strong and of a good courage; be not afraid, neither be thou dismayed: for the Lord thy God is with thee whithersoever thou goest. Joshua 1:9, KJV.

If I say, "My foot slips," Your mercy, O Lord, will hold me up. In the multitude of my anxieties within me, Your comforts delight my soul. Psalms 94:18, 19, NKJV.

In You, O Lord, I seek refuge; do not let me ever be put to shame; in Your righteousness deliver me. Incline Your ear to me; rescue me speedily. Be a rock of refuge for me, a strong fortress to save me. You are indeed my rock and my fortress; for Your name's sake lead me and guide me, take me out of the net that is hidden for me, for You are my refuge. Into Your hand I commit my spirit; You have redeemed me, O Lord, faithful God. Psalms 31:1–5, NRSV.

Come unto Me, all ye that labour and are heavy laden, and I will give you rest. Take My yoke upon you, and learn of Me; for I am meek and lowly in heart: and ye shall find rest unto your souls. For My yoke is easy, and My burden is light. Matthew 11:28–30, KJV.

But You, Lord, are a shield around me, my glory, the One who lifts my head high. I call out to the Lord, and He answers me from His holy mountain. I lie down and sleep; I awake again, because the Lord sustains me. I will not fear though tens of thousands assail me on every side. Psalms 3:3–6, NIV.

What shall we then say to these things? If God be for us, who can be against us? Romans 8:31, KJV.

When I am afraid, I put my trust in You. Psalms 56:3, NIV.

Chapter 18: The Day Which Is Coming Shall Burn Them Up

"For behold, the day is coming, burning like an oven, and all the proud, yes, all who do wickedly will be stubble. And the day which is coming shall burn them up," Says the Lord of hosts, "That will leave them neither root nor branch. But to you who fear My name The Sun of Righteousness shall arise With healing in His wings; And you shall go out And grow fat like stall-fed calves. You shall trample the wicked, For they shall be ashes under the soles of your feet On the day that I do this," says the Lord of hosts. Malachi 4:1–3, NKJV.

Do not marvel at this; for the hour is coming in which all who are in the graves will hear His voice and come forth—those who have done good, to the resurrection of life, and those who have done evil, to the resurrection of condemnation. John 5:28, 29, NKJV.

The Day Which Is Coming Shall Burn Them Up ◆ 77

I indeed baptize you with water unto repentance: but He that cometh after me is mightier than I, whose shoes I am not worthy to bear: He shall baptize you with the Holy Ghost, and with fire: Whose fan is in His hand, and He will thoroughly purge His floor, and gather His wheat into the garner; but He will burn up the chaff with unquenchable fire. Matthew 3:11, 12, KJV.

As therefore the tares are gathered and burned in the fire; so shall it be in the end of this world. The Son of Man shall send forth His angels, and they shall gather out of His kingdom all things that offend, and them which do iniquity; And shall cast them into a furnace of fire: there shall be wailing and gnashing of teeth. Matthew 13:40–42, KJV.

But he that shall blaspheme against the Holy Ghost hath never forgiveness, but is in danger of eternal damnation. Mark 3:29, KJV.

For if God spared not the angels that sinned, but cast them down to hell, and delivered them into chains of darkness, to be reserved unto judgement. 2 Peter 2:4, KJV.

Even as Sodom and Gomorrah, and the cities about them in like manner, giving themselves over to fornication, and going after strange flesh, are set forth for an example, suffering the vengeance of eternal fire. Jude 1:7, KJV.

And then the lawless one will be revealed, whom the Lord Jesus will overthrow with the breath of His mouth and destroy by the splendor of His coming. 2 Thessalonians 2:8, NIV.

Not everyone who says to me, "Lord, Lord," will enter the kingdom of heaven, but only the one who does the will of my Father who is in heaven. Matthew 7:21, NIV.

Then shall He say also unto them on the left hand, Depart from Me, ye cursed, into everlasting fire, prepared for the devil and his angels. Matthew 25:41, KJV.

With God we will gain the victory, and He will trample down our enemies. Psalms 60:12, NIV.

But go and learn what this means: "I desire mercy and not sacrifice." For I did not come to call the righteous, but sinners, to repentance. Matthew 9:13, NKJV.

And we want each one of you to show the same diligence so as to realize the full assurance of hope to the very end, so that you may not become sluggish, but imitators of those who through faith and patience inherit the promises. Hebrews 6:11, 12, NRSV.

The God of peace will soon crush Satan under your feet. The grace of our Lord Jesus be with you. Romans 16:20, NIV.

But the wicked will perish: Though the Lord's enemies are like the flowers of the field, they will be consumed, they will go up in smoke. Psalms 37:20, NIV.

And these shall go away into everlasting punishment: but the righteous into life eternal. Matthew 25:46, KJV.

What do you conspire against the Lord? He will make an utter end of it. Affliction will not rise up a second time. Nahum 1:9, NKJV.

And I saw thrones, and they sat upon them, and judgment was given unto them: and I saw the souls of them that were beheaded for the witness of Jesus, and for the word of God, and which had not worshiped the beast, neither his image, neither had received his mark upon their foreheads, or in their hands; and they lived and reigned with Christ a thousand years. But the rest of the dead lived not again until the thousand years were finished. This is the first resurrection. Blessed and holy is he that hath part in the first resurrection: on such the second death hath no power, but they shall be priests of God and of Christ, and shall reign with Him a thousand years. Revelation 20:4–6, KJV.

And when the thousand years are expired, Satan shall be loosed out of his prison, And shall go out to deceive the nations which are in the four quarters of the earth, Gog and Magog, to gather them together to battle: the number of whom is as the sand of the sea. And they went up on the breadth of the earth, and compassed the camp of the saints about, and the beloved city: and fire came down from God out of heaven, and devoured them. Revelation 20:7–9, KJV.

Chapter 19: Therefore Pray

In this manner, therefore, pray: Our Father in heaven, Hallowed be Your name. Your kingdom come. Your will be done On earth as it is in heaven. Give us this day our daily bread. And forgive us our debts, As we forgive our debtors. And do not lead us into temptation, But deliver us from the evil one. For Yours is the kingdom and the power and the glory forever. Amen. Matthew 6:9–13, NKJV.

But as for me, when they were sick, My clothing was sackcloth; I humbled myself with fasting; And my prayer would return to my own heart. Psalms 35:13, NKJV.

When I heard these things, I sat down and wept. For some days I mourned and fasted and prayed before the God of heaven. Nehemiah 1:4, NIV.

If I shut up heaven that there be no rain, or if I command the locusts to devour the land, or if I send pestilence among My people; If My people, which are called by My name, shall humble themselves, and pray, and seek My face, and turn from their wicked ways; then will I hear from heaven, and will forgive their sin, and will heal their land. 2 Chronicles 7:13, 14, KJV.

For "Those who desire life and desire to see good days, let them keep their tongues from evil and their lips from speaking deceit; let them turn away from evil and do good; let them seek peace and pursue it. For the eyes of the Lord are on the righteous, and His ears are open to their prayer. But the face of the Lord is against those who do evil." 1 Peter 3:10–12, NRSV.

For where two or three are gathered together in My name, there am I in the midst of them. Matthew 18:20, KJV.

Watch and pray, lest you enter into temptation. The spirit indeed is willing, but the flesh is weak. Matthew 26:41, NKJV.

The angel of the Lord encampeth round about them that fear Him, and delivereth them. Psalms 34:7, KJV.

The righteous cry out, and the Lord hears them; He delivers them from all their troubles. The Lord is close to the brokenhearted and saves those who are crushed in spirit. Psalms 34:17, 18, NIV.

For this reason I bow my knees to the Father of our Lord Jesus Christ, from whom the whole family in heaven and earth is named. Ephesians 3:14, 15, NKJV.

At the evening sacrifice I arose from my fasting; and having torn my garment and my robe, I fell on my knees and spread out my hands to the Lord my God. And I said: "O my God, I am too ashamed and humiliated to lift up my face to You, my God; for our iniquities have risen higher than our heads, and our guilt has grown up to the heavens." Ezra 9:5, 6, NKJV.

O come, let us worship and bow down: let us kneel before the Lord our Maker. Psalms 95:6, KJV.

Until now you have not asked for anything in My name. Ask and you will receive, and your joy will be complete. John 16:24, NIV.

Heal me, LORD, and I will be healed; save me and I will be saved, for you are the one I praise. Jeramiah 17:14, NIV.

For I know the thoughts that I think toward you, says the Lord, thoughts of peace and not of evil, to give you a future and a hope. Then you will call upon Me and go and pray to Me, and I will listen to you. And you will seek Me and find Me, when you search for Me with all your heart. Jeremiah 29:11-13, NKJV.

Jesus answered them, "Truly I tell you, if you have faith and do not doubt, not only will you do what has been done to the fig tree, but even if you say to this mountain, 'Be lifted up and thrown into the sea,' it will be done. Whatever you ask for in prayer with faith, you will receive." Matthew 21:21, 22, NRSV.

I urge, then, first of all, that petitions, prayers, intercession and thanksgiving be made for all people—for kings and all those in authority, that we may live peaceful and quiet lives in all godliness and holiness. This is good, and pleases God our Savior, who wants all people to be saved and to come to a knowledge of the truth. 1 Timothy 2:1–4, NIV.

Ask and it will be given to you; seek and you will find; knock and the door will be opened to you. For everyone who asks receives; the one who seeks finds; and to the one who knocks, the door will be opened. If you, then, though you are evil, know how to give good gifts to your children, how much more will your Father in heaven give good gifts to those who ask Him! So in everything, do to others what you would have them do to you, for this sums up the Law and the Prophets. Matthew 7:7, 8, 11, 12, NIV.

If you abide in Me, and My words abide in you, you will ask what you desire, and it shall be done for you. By this My Father is glorified, that you bear much fruit; so you will be My disciples. John 15:7, 8, NKJV.

I, even I, am He that blotteth out thy transgressions for Mine own sake, and will not remember thy sins. Isaiah 43:25, KJV.

And whatever you ask in My name, that I will do, that the Father may be glorified in the Son. John 14:13, NKJV.

While I was speaking and praying, confessing my sin and the sin of my people Israel and making my request to the Lord my God for His holy hill. Daniel 9:20, NIV.

And Cornelius said, Four days ago I was fasting until this hour; and at the ninth hour I prayed in my house, and, behold, a man stood before me in bright clothing, And said, Cornelius, thy prayer has been heard, and thine alms are had in remembrance in the sight of God. Acts 10:30, 31, KJV.

Call unto Me, and I will answer thee, and shew thee great and mighty things, which thou knowest not. Jeremiah 33:3, KJV.

And this is the confidence that we have in Him, that, if we ask any thing according to His will, He heareth us: And if we know that He hear us, whatsoever we ask, we know that we have the petitions that we desired of Him. 1 John 5:14, 15, KJV.

Then He said to His disciples, "The harvest truly is plentiful, but the laborers are few. Therefore pray the Lord of the harvest to send out laborers into His harvest." Matthew 9:37, 38, NKJV.

Chapter 20: He Is Coming with Clouds

Behold, He is coming with clouds, and every eye will see Him, even they who pierced Him. And all the tribes of the earth will mourn because of Him. Even so, Amen. Revelation 1:7, NKJV.

Let not your heart be troubled; you believe in God, believe also in Me. In My Father's house are many mansions; if it were not so, I would have told you. I go to prepare a place for you. And if I go and prepare a place for you, I will come again and receive you to Myself; that where I am, there you may be also. John 14:1–3, NKJV.

Who also said, "Men of Galilee, why do you stand gazing up into heaven? This same Jesus, who was taken up from you into heaven, will so come in like manner as you saw Him go into heaven." Acts 1:11, NKJV.

So Christ was once offered to bear the sins of many; and unto them that look for Him shall He appear the second time without sin unto salvation. Hebrews 9:28, KJV.

For I know that my Redeemer lives, And He shall stand at last on the earth; And after my skin is destroyed, this I know, That in my flesh I shall see God, Whom I shall see for myself, And my eyes shall behold, and not another. How my heart yearns within me! Job 19:25–27, NKJV.

But our citizenship is in heaven. And we eagerly await a Savior from there, the Lord Jesus Christ, who, by the power that enables Him to bring everything under His control, will transform our lowly bodies so that they will be like His glorious body. Philippians 3:20, 21, NIV.

Behold, what manner of love the Father hath bestowed upon us, that we should be called the sons of God: therefore the world knoweth us not, because it knew Him not. Beloved, now are we the sons of God, and it doth not yet appear what we shall be: but we know that, when He shall appear, we shall be like Him; for we shall see Him as He is. 1 John 3:1, 2, KJV.

But as it is written, Eye hath not seen, nor ear heard, neither have entered into the heart of man, the things which God hath prepared for them that love Him." 1 Corinthians 2:9, KJV.

For we were saved in this hope, but hope that is seen is not hope; for why does one still hope for what he sees? But if we hope for what we do not see, we eagerly wait for it with perseverance. Romans 8:24, 25, NKJV.

Truly my soul silently waits for God; From Him comes my salvation. He only is my rock and my salvation; He is my defense; I shall not be greatly moved. Psalms 62:1, 2, NKJV.

For, behold, I create new heavens and a new earth: and the former shall not be remembered, nor come into mind. And I will rejoice in Jerusalem, and joy in My people: and the voice of weeping shall be no more heard in her, nor the voice of crying. Isaiah 65:17,19, KJV.

Therefore the redeemed of the Lord shall return, and come with singing unto Zion; and everlasting joy shall be upon their head: they shall obtain gladness and joy; and sorrow and mourning shall flee away. Isaiah 51:11, KJV.

He will swallow up death in victory; and the Lord God will wipe away tears from off all faces; and the rebuke of His people shall He take away from off all the earth: for the Lord hath spoken it. And it shall be said in that day, Lo, this is our God; we have waited for Him, and He will save us:

this is the Lord; we have waited for Him, we will be glad and rejoice in His salvation. Isaiah 25:8, 9, KJV.

Him that overcometh will I make a pillar in the temple of My God, and he shall go no more out: and I will write upon him the name of My God, and the name of the city of My God, which is New Jerusalem, which cometh down out of heaven from My God: and I will write upon him My new name. Revelation 3:12, KJV.

What is man that You are mindful of him, And the son of man that You visit him? For You have made him a little lower than the angels, And You have crowned him with glory and honor. You have made him to have dominion over the works of Your hands; You have put all things under his feet, All sheep and oxen—Even the beasts of the field, The birds of the air, And the fish of the sea That pass through the paths of the seas. Psalms 8:4–8, NKJV.

Then will the eyes of the blind be opened and the ears of the deaf unstopped. Then will the lame leap like a deer, and the mute tongue shout for joy. Water will gush forth in the wilderness and streams in the desert. The burning sand will become a pool, the thirsty ground bubbling springs. In the haunts where jackals once lay, grass and reeds and papyrus will grow. And a highway will be there; it will be called the Way of Holiness; it will be for those who walk on that Way. The unclean will not journey on it; wicked fools will not go about on it. No lion will be there, nor any ravenous beast; they will not be found there. But only the redeemed will walk there, and those the Lord has rescued will return. They will enter Zion with singing; everlasting joy will crown their heads. Gladness and joy will overtake them, and sorrow and sighing will flee away. Isaiah 35:5–10, NIV.

They will build houses and dwell in them; they will plant vineyards and eat their fruit. No longer will they build houses and others live in them, or plant and others eat. For as the days of a tree, so will be the days of My people; My chosen ones will long enjoy the work of their hands. They will not labor in vain, nor will they bear children doomed for misfortune; for they will be a people blessed by the Lord, they and their descendants with them. Isaiah 65:21–23, NIV.

"The wolf and the lamb will feed together, and the lion will eat straw like the ox, and dust will be the serpent's food. They will neither harm nor destroy on all My holy mountain," says the Lord. Isaiah 65:25, NIV.

There the wicked cease from troubling; and there the weary be at rest. There the prisoners rest together; they hear not the voice of the oppressor.

The small and great are there; and the servant is free from his master. Job 3:17–19, KJV.

And I saw as it were a sea of glass mingled with fire: and them that had gotten the victory over the beast, and over his image, and over his mark, and over the number of his name, stand on the sea of glass, having the harps of God. Revelation 15:2, KJV.

Therefore they shall come and sing in the height of Zion, and shall flow together to the goodness of the Lord, for wheat, and for wine, and for oil, and for the young of the flock and of the herd: and their soul shall be as a watered garden; and they shall not sorrow any more at all. Then shall the virgin rejoice in the dance, both young men and old together: for I will turn their mourning into joy, and will comfort them, and make them rejoice from their sorrow. Jeremiah 31:12, 13, KJV.

Knowing this first: that scoffers will come in the last days, walking according to their own lusts, and saying, "Where is the promise of His coming? For since the fathers fell asleep, all things continue as they were from the beginning of creation." For this they willfully forget: that by the word of God the heavens were of old, and the earth standing out of water and in the water, by which the world that then existed perished, being flooded with water. But the heavens and the earth which are now preserved by the same word, are reserved for fire until the day of judgment and perdition of ungodly men. But, beloved, do not forget this one thing, that with the Lord one day is as a thousand years, and a thousand years as one day. The Lord is not slack concerning His promise, as some count slackness, but is longsuffering toward us, not willing that any should perish but that all should come to repentance. 2 Peter 3:3–9, NKJV.

For you yourselves know perfectly that the day of the Lord so comes as a thief in the night. For when they say, "Peace and safety!" then sudden destruction comes upon them, as labor pains upon a pregnant woman. And they shall not escape. 1 Thessalonians 5:2, 3, NKJV.

For the vision is yet for an appointed time, but at the end it shall speak, and not lie: though it tarry, wait for it; because it will surely come, it will not tarry. Habakkuk 2:3, KJV.

But of that day and hour knoweth no man, no, not the angels of heaven, but My Father only. Matthew 24:36, KJV.

But the day of the Lord will come like a thief. The heavens will disappear with a roar; the elements will be destroyed by fire, and the earth and everything done in it will be laid bare. Since everything will be destroyed in this way, what kind of people ought you to be? You ought to live holy and godly lives as you look forward to the day of God and speed its coming. That day will bring about the destruction of the heavens by fire, and the elements will melt in the heat. But in keeping with His promise we are looking forward to a new heaven and a new earth, where righteousness dwells. 2 Peter 3:10–13, NIV.

The Revelation of Jesus Christ, which God gave Him to show His servants—things which must shortly take place. And He sent and signified it by His angel to His servant John, who bore witness to the word of God, and to the testimony of Jesus Christ, to all things that he saw. Blessed is he who reads and those who hear the words of this prophecy, and keep those things which are written in it; for the time is near. Revelation 1:1–3, NKJV.

And there shall be signs in the sun, and in the moon, and in the stars; and upon the earth distress of nations, with perplexity; the sea and the waves roaring; Men's hearts failing them for fear, and for looking after those things which are coming on the earth: for the powers of heaven shall be shaken. And then shall they see the Son of Man coming in a cloud with power and great glory. And when these things begin to come to pass, then look up, and lift up your heads; for your redemption draweth nigh. Luke 21:25–28, KJV.

Be patient, then, brothers and sisters, until the Lord's coming. See how the farmer waits for the land to yield its valuable crop, patiently waiting for the autumn and spring rains. You too, be patient and stand firm, because the Lord's coming is near. Don't grumble against one another, brothers and sisters, or you will be judged. The Judge is standing at the door! Brothers and sisters, as an example of patience in the face of suffering, take the prophets who spoke in the name of the Lord. As you know, we count as blessed those who have persevered. You have heard of Job's perseverance and have seen what the Lord finally brought about. The Lord is full of compassion and mercy. James 5:7–11, NIV.

Then the sign of the Son of Man will appear in heaven, and then all the tribes of the earth will mourn, and they will see the Son of Man coming on the clouds of heaven with power and great glory. And He will send His angels with a great sound of a trumpet, and they will gather together His elect from the four winds, from one end of heaven to the other. Now learn this parable from the fig tree: When its branch has already become tender and puts forth leaves, you know that summer is near. So you also, when you see all these things, know that it is near—at the doors! Matthew 24:30–33, NKJV.

And behold, I am coming quickly, and My reward is with Me, to give to every one according to his work. I am the Alpha and the Omega, the Beginning and the End, the First and the Last. Revelation 22:12, 13, NKJV.

And I heard a loud voice from heaven saying, "Behold, the tabernacle of God is with men, and He will dwell with them, and they shall be His people. God Himself will be with them and be their God. And God will wipe away every tear from their eyes; there shall be no more death, nor sorrow, nor crying. There shall be no more pain, for the former things have passed away." Revelation 21:3, 4, NKJV.

He who testifies to these things says, "Surely I am coming quickly." Amen. Even so, come, Lord Jesus! The grace of our Lord Jesus Christ be with you all. Amen. Revelation 22:20, 21, NJKV.

TEACH Services, Inc.
PUBLISHING

We invite you to view the complete
selection of titles we publish at:
www.TEACHServices.com

We encourage you to write us
with your thoughts about this,
or any other book we publish at:
info@TEACHServices.com

TEACH Services' titles may be purchased in
bulk quantities for educational, fund-raising,
business, or promotional use.
bulksales@TEACHServices.com

Finally, if you are interested in seeing
your own book in print, please contact us at:
publishing@TEACHServices.com
We are happy to review your manuscript at no charge.

www.ingramcontent.com/pod-product-compliance
Lightning Source LLC
Chambersburg PA
CBHW042133160426
43199CB00021B/2895